WILD EAST

WILD EAST

TRAVELS IN THE NEW MONGOLIA

JILL LAWLESS

SUMMERSDALE

First published by ECW Press in 2000.

This edition published in 2002 by Summersdale Publishers Ltd.

Summersdale Publishers Ltd
46 West Street
Chichester
West Sussex
PO19 1RP
UK

www.summersdale.com

Printed and bound in Great Britain.

ISBN 1 84024 210 8

Front cover images © David South and Liz Lawless.

About the Author

Canadian journalist Jill Lawless gave up a job as a big-city theatre critic to edit the *UB Post*, a fledgling independent newspaper in newly democratic Mongolia. She has written on Mongolia for Agence France-Presse, *The Guardian*, the *Far Eastern Economic Review*, Deutsche Welle radio, and the Canadian Broadcasting Corporation, and has ridden a horse, a camel, but not, alas, a yak. She works as a journalist in London.

for my mother and father

Acknowledgements

Thanks are due to my colleagues at the *UB Post* and the Mongol News Company, especially Ts. Baldorj, Ts. Jargalsaikhan, A. Delgermaa, N. Oyunbayar, Z. Zolzaya, S. Erdenebileg, G. Bodibilguun, and D. Bat-Erdene, for their invaluable help and support while I was in Mongolia. I would also like to thank everyone I interviewed, from herders to Members of Parliament for their time and openness.

Many people in Ulaanbaatar provided friendship, sustenance, and an endless supply of stories; in particular I'd like to thank Rob, Julie, Chris, Orna, Annette, Michael, Damien, Jerry, Pie and Hans, Laurenz and Anke, Ariunbat, Chimgee, Brian and Tuya, and the staff of Millie's café.

In memoriam: Matthew Girvin, B. Bayarmaa and Michael Frank.

Elsewhere in Asia, Leslie Chang, David McIntyre and Thomas Crampton supplied much-appreciated hospitality.

My thanks go to the manufacturers of the sturdy Russian jeep and the Toyota Landcruiser, and my admiration and gratitude to the drivers who pilot them across Mongolia's unforgiving roads.

Some of the material in this book originated in pieces I did for Agence France-Presse, Deutsche Welle, the *Far Eastern Economic Review*, *The Guardian* and CBC Radio's This Morning; thanks to all of them.

Thanks too, to everyone at Summersdale.

Finally, my thanks and love go to my husband, David South, a born adventurer, without whom this book would not have been written.

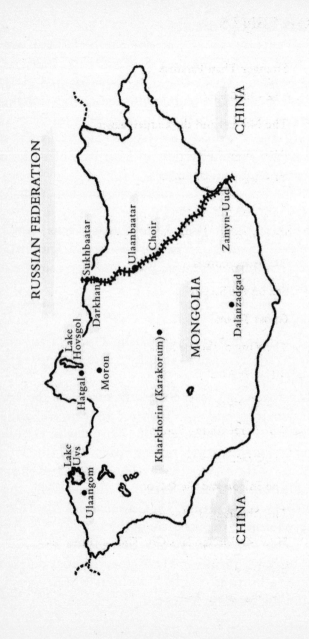

CONTENTS

Chapter One

Stranger Than Paradise

I first glimpsed Mongolia in summer, from the air. The overwhelming impression was of space, beauty – and a deceptive serenity.

I flew to Ulaanbaatar from Beijing. We climbed through smog and over a landscape of black and brown but began our descent toward a green and inviting world: a gently undulating sea of rich grass, flecked with white dots, like aspirin scattered over a green bedspread.

These white dots – the round, canvas-covered, felt tents called *gers* that have been home to Mongolia's nomadic herders since time immemorial – were almost the only signs of human life. I couldn't see the city we were approaching. I made out one thin stretch of paved road, entirely free of cars.

The view fit perfectly with my half-formed impressions of this wild and open country. Naturally, I was thrilled.

On the ground, I discovered, things are a lot rougher.

This realisation came to me four days later, when I found myself sitting by the side of a broken-down Russian van in the middle of the Gobi desert, huddled beside a flaming pile of camel dung, singing Finnish campfire songs and chewing on tinned sardines. My *Lost Horizon*, I mused bitterly, had turned into a Jim Jarmusch film that went on forever. (Arguably, that's every Jarmusch film, but you get my point.)

Until that moment, every discomfort, rough edge and

outcrop of ugliness – the hideous power plant and flaking concrete buildings, the billowing soot and exposed asbestos, the ratty *ger* suburbs with their absence of planning or plumbing – had seemed to confirm the country's rugged glamour.

Ulaanbaatar was a scruffy and pitted city with a raffish Eastern European centre of blocky government edifices, tree-lined streets and pastel-painted blocks of flats, ringed by a sprawling periphery of dusty *ger* districts that straggled into the surrounding hills. And beyond that, visible from every corner, the larch-clad hills and endless grasslands.

It all enhanced my two preconceived notions of Mongolia: a land of horse-riding nomads with an occasional penchant for bloody world domination, and a secretive Communist state whose time had run out. There were the rattletrap Ladas and the statue of a lecturing Lenin in front of the Ulaanbaatar Hotel, and there were the horsemen in traditional robes trotting across Sukhbaatar Square and the portraits of Genghis Khan, whom I soon learned to call Chinggis Khan, as the Mongolians did. Both aspects seemed equally exotic.

Then I went on the road with the Finns.

There were three of them: two middle-aged women, friends, and one teenage daughter. All were blonde, and at least a couple were called Paivi. Veterans of remote and exotic destinations (in that Nordic way), they'd decided the Gobi desert in summertime was the ultimate in adventure travel.

They were hardy and resourceful. When I met them one night at the Café de France, Ulaanbaatar's premier expat hangout (chewy steak, spotty service, lovely pastries), they had already arranged a vehicle and driver to take them the 340 miles to Dalanzadgad – Seventy Springs, the capital of South Gobi province and first in a long series of cruelly disappointing Mongolian place names. A day and a half's drive each way, four days of exploring the cliffs, dunes, mountains and fossil sites of the Gobi. They had room for another passenger; I invited myself along.

The next morning, we met up outside their guest house, a flat in a pockmarked block behind the Central Post Office. I was introduced to our driver, Batbold, a wiry, taciturn man with a drooping moustache, muscular forearms, and a bullet-grey Russian van.

Our first stop was one of the city's ubiquitous battered tin kiosks. Primed by my Lonely Planet guide's warnings of food shortages, I'd been surprised to discover that the residents of Mongolia's capital are well supplied with snack food, beverages and cigarettes. But most of what makes it into the country is the cheapest, nastiest stuff: rancid Chinese Marlboros, Disko-brand filled biscuits and an abhorrent concoction known as Three-in-One (instant coffee, non-dairy creamer and sugar in a single-serving foil packet).

Stocked up with Disko biscuits, two-litre bottles of mystery-berry fizzy drink and Vietnamese sugar-coated peanuts, we set off. Inside the van, the walls and ceiling were padded. A nice touch, but a bad sign.

We drove along the paved airport road leading westward out of town. After half an hour, Batbold eased the van off the road and onto a pocked and rutted dirt track headed south across the open steppe. A shortcut, I thought. I was wrong. This was the road.

The rest of the day was like riding a roller coaster designed by a sadist: endless hours of bouncing and swerving, during which I learned two things. Mongolia (my guidebook informed me) is the size of Western Europe but has only 750 miles of paved roads. And Mongolians are almost preternaturally patient people. I decided the two things must be related.

We were heading south, toward China. None of the paved roads runs that way. Several go to Russia. Those two things are connected too.

The Finns and I tried to chat, our heads making frequent contact with the padded ceiling. Batbold never spoke. Driving in Mongolia, I realised, requires absolute concentration. I also understood the origin of those muscular arms: Batbold wrestled with that steering wheel, as hour after hour he bullied the van over hill and across valley, chain-smoking and humming along to a wavering tape of Mongolian folk songs.

Outside, the blue sky filled three-quarters of the view, and the green landscape grew browner and dustier. Herds of camels emerged to mingle with the cows, goats, sheep and horses, diligently nosing ever thinner and more far-flung patches of grass.

Things were going well. We were averaging more than 20 miles an hour, excellent progress for the countryside. The scale of the landscape was daunting – so much rock and sky, so few people – but Batbold, quiet and self-contained, was a reassuring presence.

Then, as the colour began to leach from the gigantic

sky, we hit a rock. After a crack, a thump (my head against the ceiling), and a shudder, we were in a ditch.

We toppled out and had a look. The front axle was bent at an alarming angle.

'Oh, great,' I said, annoyed and a bit worried. We were in the middle of a nowhere of sand and craggy rock. We hadn't passed a *ger* in an hour or another vehicle in three. There were animals out here! I only had a single pack of cigarettes.

Batbold looked at the damage and sucked a sibilant rush of air through his teeth. From the van he took a jack and a huge oily bag full of greasy tools and bits of vehicle. Then he set to work, hammering, filing, and building a small fire to heat and bend bits of metal. Still he didn't say a word.

The Finns and I watched for a while as the pile of parts on the ground grew so large it occurred to me Batbold might be trying to build a whole new vehicle.

This was obviously going to take a while, and it was getting dark. I sat on a rock and lit a cigarette with chilled fingers. The Finns kicked into action.

'Right,' said one of the Paivis. 'There was a well about half a mile back. I'm going for water.' And she and the teenager, Jenni, disappeared with our empty bottles.

The other Paivi looked at me. 'We should build a fire. We will have to burn dung, as the nomads do.'

I'd no idea that's what the nomads did, but since there wasn't a tree for miles I believed her.

I shuffled around gathering dusty cakes of (mercifully odourless) camel droppings, which Paivi stacked into a neat pyramid. It burned immediately and cleanly.

The others returned with bottles of clear water and unpacked a small saucepan from a dayglo knapsack. They put water on for tea, and we spread our remaining food supplies on the ground: a packet of Disko biscuits, half a loaf of bread, a tin of sardines. Paivi produced a wire coat-hanger (a coat-hanger!) that she unfurled into a skewer; she toasted bread for sardine sandwiches.

Batbold kept up his chorus of clinks and pings. He took his sardine on toast silently and ate it without stopping his work.

I ate my sandwich and two biscuits, drank my tea, and felt marginally less miserable and cold. I tried not to think about (a) the limits of Batbold's mechanical skills, (b) the rare but still worrisome Gobi bear, and (c) the lack of any passing vehicles in the two hours we had been there.

The Finns didn't seem worried; they were just warming up. From deep in a knapsack they produced a bottle of vodka – a gift for the herding family with whom we were supposed to be spending the night. Paivi poured it into a plastic bottle a third full of grapefruit fizzy drink and shook it vigorously. The other Paivi passed me a weather-beaten notebook.

'Campfire songs!' she said triumphantly. She flicked through the pages. 'I think you have this song in English, yes? '500 Miles'?'

The sardines turned to ash in my mouth – not, admittedly, that far a journey.

I must have dozed. I think it was the ceasing of Batbold's clinking, rather than the Finnish-language rendition of 'Kumbaya,' that startled me awake.

In the flickering firelight, I saw Batbold stand up stiffly, black all over with oil and dirt. I raised an eyebrow quizzically. He nodded slightly. The van was fixed.

I could have hugged him. But I am Canadian, and he is Mongolian, so with nice northern reserve I just said *bayarlalaa* – thanks – and handed him the glass of fizzy grapefruit vodka we'd saved for him. He drank it slowly, washed his hands and face with the dregs of a bottle of water, and lay down on the ground to sleep. It was 4 a.m. This, I thought, was a great glimpse of the Mongolian character: self-sufficient, hardy, stoic, resourceful. No wonder the Mongols won an empire.

In the morning, Batbold – clean and seemingly untired – got back behind the wheel, and we continued our journey south.

Then two things happened. The first was that, after 15 minutes and perhaps three miles, we broke down again. There was a metallic snap, a thump, and we were still. This time our situation was far more serious. We were miles from the well, and it would soon be midday. There was no shade.

Batbold repeated his strategy, setting methodically to work on the van. The Finns and I muttered nervously. We decided that two of us would go for help. Somewhere nearby there *must* be a ger (we hoped); perhaps the family would have a truck. At least they would have horses on which to ride to the nearest wealthy homestead.

The Paivis set off, armed with a compass and one of our last two bottles of well water, promising not to go too far or get lost.

I flopped down in the dirt and reflected on our situation. The land stretched flat and beige in all directions. There were no signs of human life as far as the eye could see, and that was a long way – so far that I almost imagined I could see the ocean. Eventually I decided that the pink-brown smudge on the horizon was a distant mountain range. Up close, the dusty earth was surprisingly fertile, sprouting clumps of thin grass. I took an exploratory nibble. Chives. Well, that's something, I thought.

We would be all right. People did live in this land; we would find help. We would just have to remain still and be patient.

After an hour or so, Batbold emerged from under the van. He did look drained this time. He climbed into the cab. The engine turned over; it started. I felt a pang of relief tinged with anxiety.

Then the second thing happened. *Batbold started to drive off.* I poked my head over the front seat.

'Where are you going?' I gasped. 'Paivi . . .'

Batbold indicated with a sweep of his arm that we were going to look for them.

This, I thought, was a very bad idea. I remonstrated in high-pitched English; he ignored me with eloquent Mongolian silence. We drove tentatively toward what Batbold had spotted as a slight rise in the seemingly flat land, a small scree-covered hill. At its crest he climbed out, surveyed the land all around, then set off again. He repeated this process three times. Each time I looked in vain for a flash of white, a puff of smoke, anything. I saw nothing. Batbold proceeded methodically until, at last, a white dot appeared in the far, far distance.

'*Ger*!' I exclaimed, pointing. Batbold gave the slightest nod. He'd seen it long before I had.

The *ger* sat alone in the shelter of some large rocks. A young man in tracksuit bottoms and a Chicago Bulls T-shirt and an old woman in a purple robe called a *del* stood outside, observing our juddering approach. Batbold climbed out, wiped a forearm across his brow, said a laconic hello, and began a terse summation of our troubles.

'Paivi,' I said, tugging at his sleeve, sweeping my hand across the sun-baked emptiness in which, somewhere, two Finns were wandering. 'Do they have a truck?'

Batbold asked the young man, who shook his head. No truck. Instead, he saddled up a horse and struck out in search of the Paivis.

The old woman plucked a tray of hard cubes of curd from the roof of the *ger*, where they were drying, ushered us inside, sat us down, decanted the curds into a bowl, passed it around and ladled out bowls of salty milk tea. I popped one of the acrid curds into my mouth, gagging only slightly, and tried to soften it up with mouthfuls of tea. The old woman set a blackened wok on the stove and began to cook as we sat, too tired and hungry to chat. After 30 minutes or so, she presented us each with a tin plate of noodles mixed with mutton and a few shards of onion. Ravenous, I started to shovel the food down, choking on the tough, gamey meat and globs of fat. The woman regarded her foreign guests for a moment, went and rummaged around in a cupboard, and returned with a small bottle, which she pressed into my hand. It was soy sauce. I could have wept with gratitude.

Just as we'd finished our meal and begun to slip into a daze, we heard the sound of hooves and a high-pitched engine. We pressed through the door and saw, in a cloud of dust, the young man on his horse, accompanied by a porkpie-hatted herder on a green Russian motorbike, with the two Paivis perched precariously on the back.

There was a chorus of low-key greetings and congratulations. Batbold's moustache seemed to droop a bit less; for a man who had not seemed worried, he looked suspiciously relieved.

'Where the hell did you go?' fumed a Paivi. 'We found a *ger*, and a motorcycle, and went back to get you – and you were gone!'

'It wasn't me,' I said, past caring, awash with relief. 'It was Batbold. He wanted to go and look for you. I couldn't persuade him. It's his van.' It's his country, his logic, his plan. 'Anyway, it all worked out in the end.'

'I'm not so sure,' said Jenni. 'I'm afraid the van might still be broken.'

Batbold and the men were conferring. After a few minutes, he came over to us and managed to convey his plan. We would spend the night at the *ger*; there was a gold mine nearby, the only place for miles with electricity, and in the morning he'd go there and fix the van properly.

It was an excellent plan, we all agreed. Exhausted, we pitched our sleeping bags in the gravel by the side of the *ger* and went to sleep.

I was awakened at dawn by the pitiful, otherworldly mewling of baby camels crying for their mothers. Batbold and the van were already gone, in search of electricity. The harsh desert landscape was softened, friendly in the gentle dawn light: the sky was azure blue giving way to creeping orange, and the distant mountains to the west were a splash of pink on the horizon.

We ate a breakfast of milky rice pudding, then walked half a mile to the nearest well. It was a cement-lined hole in the ground with a wooden cover, and beside it stood a rubber bucket on a pole and a long trough. Built and maintained in Communist times, it was now crumbling and chipping away. We were alone in the pure early-morning light, but when we plunged the bucket in, hauled it up, and sloshed some water into the trough, animals began to materialise. First a herd of horses, lining up in neat rows on either side of the trough, then behind them a jostling crowd of sheep and goats, waiting their turn.

When all the animals had retired, sated, we filled all our bottles, stripped off, produced bars of soap, and rinsed away the Gobi, pouring the icy water over our heads with shudders of pleasure.

When we got back to the *ger*, Batbold had returned with the man of the house, two friends from the mine, their wives and seven or eight small children. We crowded into the *ger* to celebrate our success. First came bowls of *airag* – fermented mare's milk, sharp and fizzy and the strength of weak beer – and then the man of the house produced an old green bottle from which he poured a cloudy liquid into a small silver bowl. Each guest received the bowl in turn – beginning with Batbold, hero of the hour – and downed the liquid in a neat gulp. This was homemade vodka, distilled like *airag* from mare's milk. It shot down with a sharp vodka tang and then settled with a disquieting dairy aftertaste.

When the bottle was empty, someone produced a bottle of real, shop-bought vodka.

'Shouldn't we get going?' I said, making steering-wheel-twisting motions at Batbold. 'We're two days behind schedule already.'

He nodded. Straight away. We'd just finish the vodka, then take a few photos.

Sure, that was OK. Of course they'd want family photos. No problem. The vodka consumed, we trooped outside, while the family groups combed their hair, straightened their hats, and stood to attention in various combinations for family photos. Then a few more: the men exchanging snuff bottles. The men wrestling. The men astride the motorbike. The boys wrestling. The children on horseback.

An hour and five rolls of film later, we finally took our leave. We climbed into the van and waved. The children clambered onto the rear bumper. The adults stuck their heads through the windows with last-minute requests and lengthy farewells. There was a tangle of arms, a clamour of voices. It was like the departure of a troop ship. Finally, we pulled away, waving maniacally, children leaping off the back of the van. The old woman emerged from the *ger* with a saucepan; with a flick of her wrist and a shout of '*Sain yavararai*' – go well – she covered our rear window with milk.

In the back of the van, the Finns were conferring in Finnish. 'We think maybe we should head back to Ulaanbaatar. We are almost two days behind schedule now. What if the van breaks down again? We could miss our plane.'

We put the suggestion to Batbold. He looked offended. We had paid to go to Dalanzadgad, and to Dalanzadgad we would go. We hadn't even seen the sand-dunes yet, or the Flaming Cliffs, where archaeologists had made some of the world's richest finds of dinosaur fossils, or Eagle Valley, a mountain gorge with a river that remained frozen, even in summer. We had been promised those things, and we would see them. We couldn't turn back now.

And so we drove. And drove and drove. The next morning, four days after leaving Ulaanbaatar, we reached Dalanzadgad, a dusty, low-slung straggle of a town, and after a brief stop to buy petrol from the petrol station and chocolate and tomatoes from the market, we drove on. We finally reached the mountains, drove up a winding path and down into a rocky cleft of a valley, hiked up the gorge, and discovered that the river was . . . water.

'It used to be frozen all year round,' said the apologetic park ranger, a big, bluff man in a baseball cap. 'But now the ice melts in July and August. We're very worried about it. We think it may be global warming and also the impact of tourists walking on the ice and breaking it up. But we have a project to address the problem. We have received some money from the United Nations! We are conducting an environmental-assessment survey.'

I didn't mind. It was a lovely spot, green and rocky and watery, an alpine gorge that had somehow wandered off, got lost, and ended up in the middle of the Gobi desert. And the hills were alive with the sound of gerbils. As we walked, small brown rodents scurried through the grass ahead of us, scampering out of our way.

I could have gone home happy after that. But Batbold would not, could not, stay still. He was determined we should see everything; he was a driving machine. So after a night in the mountains, it was on to the Flaming Cliffs (red) and the sand-dunes – brown, slippery, delightfully squishy, but also a place where (and this is the voice of experience speaking) it is very easy for a van to become stuck, to spin its tyres and dig itself in to the wheel rims, to refuse to budge while its occupants push and strain and bicker and despair and burn and bake in the sun for seven hours until salvation arrives in the form of four Land Cruiser loads of strapping Australian tourists who gather, flex their muscles, count ('one, two, three, heave'), and pull you out.

So we saw the sights. And then it was the morning of the seventh day. The Finns, who had been growing increasingly anxious, finally snapped.

'Look, Batbold,' they said. 'We are supposed to be in Ulaanbaatar tonight. We are meeting friends at Café de France at eight. Our plane leaves the day after tomorrow. What are we going to do?'

Batbold regarded them phlegmatically. We all understood one another a lot better by now.

'We will drive back today,' he said. 'It's OK. It's only 300 miles.'

'But it took us four days to drive that far!'

'It's OK,' he said.

I had made a decision, against everything in my nature, to be mellow, to adjust my body clock to Mongolian Time. But I could feel shards of anxiety and frustration ripping through the façade. I looked hard at Batbold and tried to see into his soul. Was he an eternal optimist? A hopeless planner? Had he forgotten his recent history? Was he a metaphor for Mongolia? I gave up. I settled into the back of the van and prepared to drive.

And we drove. We bounced around in the back, on edge, fearing every bump would be the vehicle's last. Batbold gripped and twisted the steering wheel, eyes on the ground in front of us, and nudged the van forward. It got dark. He kept driving, navigating each small patch of ground illuminated by the headlights, one after another. We dozed. Outside, there was a distant rumble, getting louder, then a crack. I started, my stomach churned – the van! – and I looked out the window. The rumble subsided, then built up again. There was another crack, and the landscape was illuminated, a vast silver plain, and a crackling fork of lightning stabbed the ground to our left.

'Holy shit,' I said. 'It's a lightning storm. We're driving across a wafer-flat landscape, we're in a metal box, and we're the highest thing for miles around.'

Batbold kept driving. I curled into a ball, trying not to touch any metal, and eventually I fell asleep again. I didn't wake until the bump and grind of our wheels on the track were replaced by a steady rumbling. We were on a paved road.

It was four in the morning. Batbold had been driving for 20 hours. Out of the black night, a line of streetlights appeared, edging the road. The road climbed a hill, and when we reached the top we could see Ulaanbaatar spread out before us in its valley, a warm and welcoming ribbon of lights. Batbold pulled over, climbed stiffly out of the driver's seat, stretched, and wandered off to have a pee. We tumbled out, stood gawking.

'Civilisation,' said Paivi. 'Hot water . . .'

'Well, water, anyway,' I said.

'And restaurants and a soft bed.'

'Batbold, he's a hero,' said the other Paivi.

'He's an idiot,' snapped teenage Jenni.

'No,' I said, 'I reckon he's a hero too.'

Batbold reappeared, and we all shook his hand and clapped him on the back, pointing down to the city with expressions of delight. He settled back into the driver's seat, gave his moustache a little tug, and headed down the hill to town.

Chapter Two

The Outsiders

I'll give you the short version. The Mongols came thundering out of nowhere, they conquered the world, and then they went home.

That's not much of an exaggeration. In the thirteenth century, under the leadership of Chinggis Khan (Genghis to you), the Mongol armies carved out the largest contiguous land empire the world has ever known. They conquered an area stretching from Korea to Hungary, from Vietnam to Afghanistan. And they did it all within a few decades, combining the speed and seemingly superhuman stamina of their cavalry with ruthless and inventive siege tactics. They were probably the greatest shock to the system the outside world has ever known. The arrival of the sweaty horsemen must have seemed no less cataclysmic than an alien invasion.

So much so, indeed, that the image of the savage 'Mongol hordes' is almost all that remains of them in the consciousness of the outside world. (So much so, as well, that the Klingons of *Star Trek*, with their leather tunics, their warlike ways, their guttural language and their khans, are a distillation of the West's image of the Mongol.)

They are history's ultimate outsiders, saddled with the world's worst possible rap. Did they deserve it? Through their conquests, they changed the world. Did it change them? And, after all that, where did they go?

Let's start at the beginning. In ancient times, a

smattering of tribes was scattered across a cold, remote, forbidding land. They were nomads, living in felt tents and tending their herds, holding little truck with notions such as king or country. Their loyalty was to small groups: families, clans. This allegiance led to regular tribal skirmishes and wars, ad hoc alliances, frequent regroupings. Occasionally one group would gain dominance, absorbing or expelling the others – one such exiled group was the Huns, whose leader, Attila, was to give Europe so much grief – until gradually they began to think of themselves as one people: the Mongols.

It was a hard life in a hard place, especially when compared to the agriculturally rich and settled lands of China, to the south, across the Gobi desert and the Altai Mountains. So when the Chinese were weak and in disarray, and the nomads hungry, the northern tribes would attack; when China was strong, they'd retreat behind the mountains and the desert. To defend themselves against these attacks, the Chinese began to build a wall in the third century BC – the Great Wall of China. (It didn't work. As Chinggis Khan discovered, there was no need to storm the wall when you could simply bribe the guards.)

A scrappy, independent, disorganised people in conflict with China – this would characterise the Mongols for centuries to come. In the first millennium AD, a pattern emerged: a succession of Mongol tribes would rise up, conquer the others and harry the Chinese; then their alliances would fragment, and the process would begin again. Some of these tribes still exist – such as the Uighurs, a Muslim people who inhabit Xinjiang in western China – and others, such as the Khitan, do not. The ruins of their forts are still scattered across the Mongolian steppe.

The rest of the world left them to it. The Mongol homeland was a place no one had much reason to go to, so no one paid much attention to the Mongols. Certainly their neighbours to the south had a low opinion of their occasional attackers; the Chinese, with their highly developed agriculture and sophisticated civilisation, had little interest in a crowd of barbarians who could neither reap nor sow, who had no written language and little government, and who spent their time herding and drinking, with occasional tribal battles thrown in.

Then, in 1162 or so, a son was born to a family in eastern Mongolia, a boy named Temujin. His father, a clan leader, was killed when the boy was 12, and the family was cast out, abandoned. Nonetheless, through wile, charisma and force of will, the youngster rose to become a leader, first of his own clan, then of a loose federation of Mongol tribes. He assembled an army, made it the best-trained, best-organised army anyone had ever seen (it was based on a system of tens, so that one man commanded a platoon of ten, another oversaw ten platoons, all the way up to a *tumen*, a disciplined, ordered force of 10,000 men), and set about, through wars and alliances, uniting the Mongols. He succeeded.

In 1206, a *khuriltai* – a meeting of clan elders – proclaimed him Chinggis Khan, Universal King, the ruler 'of all those who live in felt tents.' He was a brilliant organiser. He established a sophisticated communications and supply network for the scattered

Mongols. He borrowed a script from the Uighurs to give Mongolia a written language, and he laid down the Mongols' first legal code.

Then Chinggis started to look outward. Maybe he wanted more than a nomad's precarious existence. Some have suggested that a series of unusually cold winters had decimated the Mongols' herds and threatened the nomads' survival. Perhaps he thought he had a divine mission, a manifest destiny. It certainly looked that way to others, for once he started the business of conquest, there was no stopping him. By 1215, he had occupied the northern Chinese capital, present-day Beijing. Then he moved west. By the 1220s, his armies were rolling over Russia, the Caucasus, modern-day Ukraine.

The people whom his armies conquered recorded the Mongols as savages of unparalleled strength and brutality. But from the start, their success depended on the support of foreigners – first on Chinese and Muslim engineers, who schooled the Mongol armies in siege warfare, later on soldiers from many lands, who were pressed into their armies, and then on advisors from China and Central Asia, who helped them learn how to rule. From the beginning, the Mongols were cannier, more open to the outside world, less apart than they seemed.

Then, on the crest of a seemingly unstoppable wave of conquest, in the middle of a campaign in China, Chinggis died. The Mongols then did one of those mystifying (to the outsider) things. They stopped everything. They turned around and bore their leader's body back to Mongolia to be buried, and the generals, on all the fronts of battle, stopped fighting and made the long journey home. Chinggis' legal code said that only a *khuriltai* could choose a new khan.

They all went home, and they buried their leader. No one knows for certain where he is buried. Legend has it that all who viewed the passing funeral cortège were put to death, and though in recent times foreign expeditions have set out to search for the great khan's tomb – where, legend also has it, Chinggis was interred with 40 young women and 40 horses – it has never been found.

The *khuriltai* met at Karakorum, the capital Chinggis had founded smack in the middle of the Mongolian steppe, and proclaimed Ogodei, one of his four sons, the new khan, and the conquests resumed: China, Korea, Central Asia, Russia. By 1241, the armies of this nation of fewer than a million people were sacking Krakow, besieging the Hungarian city of Pest, preparing to cross the Danube and head for Vienna and Venice and the cities of Western Europe.

Then Ogodei died, the Mongols withdrew once more to Karakorum to select a new khan, and Europe was spared. This pattern had the virtue of keeping Mongolia's enemies in suspense, but it also gave them time to regroup; it cost effort, time and lives.

And, inevitably perhaps, the descendants of Chinggis Khan started fighting over the spoils. It took several years of wrangling to choose a new khan, Ogodei's son Guyug. He died soon after and was succeeded by Mongke, another of Chinggis' grandsons, who promptly had several of his cousins executed for opposing him.

He wisely decided it was best to leave Europe for the moment and set about consolidating the Mongol conquests in Asia; but when he died, in 1259, his enemies got another breather.

It wasn't conquest the Mongols found difficult; it was rule. Mongke was succeeded, after an ugly civil war, by his brother Khubilai. Khubilai saw that the Mongols had to come to grips with this issue of ruling, and he did it ably. He had his grandfather's level head and skill for organisation. He moved his administrative capital to Beijing – though he did build a stately pleasure dome at Xanadu (Shengdu), in present-day Inner Mongolia; he recruited Chinese advisors; he left his cousins in charge of the Mongol territories in Russia and Central Asia; and he focused on consolidating his Chinese domains. He became a real Chinese emperor: the first emperor of the Yuan Dynasty.

His rule was in many ways an enlightened one, a period of cultural exchange and innovation. Parks, canals and grain storehouses were built or improved, paper money was brought into circulation, and a fast and efficient postal system was introduced – a Mongolian Pony Express. The size of the Mongol Empire, and its sophisticated communications network, facilitated trade between east and west, and with it came cultural and scientific exchanges. Mongols and Chinese began to visit Europe, and Marco Polo and other western emissaries began to travel to Asia.

But the longer Khubilai and his descendants stayed in China, the less control they had over – and the less interest they had in – the other parts of their vast empire.

And that included Mongolia. They became Sinocised: less Mongolian, more Chinese. There were so few of them, relative to their subjects, and their links with their Mongol culture withered when uprooted from the land that had produced it. And as their identity changed, they lost their grip.

The Yuan Dynasty did not last long. By 1368 – only 150 years after Chinggis Khan pointed his horse's nose south and began to ride – the last of Khubilai Khan's Yuan successors had been booted back across the wall to Mongolia. With the dynasty at an end, the subjugated Chinese took their revenge. They chased the Mongols back to Karakorum and destroyed it.

This pattern of disintegration and absorption repeated itself across the Mongol lands, among the khanates of western Asia and Russia, until today only traces remain of the Mongol legacy: some place names in Moscow, such as the street Arbat and the word *Kremlin*; a holiday in Poland commemorating the battle of Leignitz in 1241; and, around the world, a faint shudder at the mention of the word *Mongol*.

Back in Mongolia, the nomads resumed their traditional pattern: bouts of unity interspersed with tribal wars. A sixteenth-century Mongol king, Altan Khan, saw in Tibetan Buddhism a means of uniting his people, and he made it the state religion. In the seventeenth century, the first Bogd Khan, a Living Buddha or god-king, was proclaimed.

The Mongols were left with their livestock and their faith, but their neighbours were growing more powerful. The Chinese from the south and the Russians from the north began to expand, applying pressure on the Mongolian homelands. The Mongolians have been squeezed between them ever since. By the eighteenth century, the Russians had taken over and begun to absorb the Buryat Mongols in the north, and in China the Manchus – originally nomads themselves – had taken control of the country, founded the Qing Dynasty, and gained control of Mongolia.

The Chinese eventually absorbed southern Mongolia – the present-day Chinese province of Inner Mongolia. The rest they mostly ignored, making sure only that the Mongolians remained indebted to the Manchu tax collectors, merchants and moneylenders.

Western travellers who visited Mongolia in the nineteenth century wrote of a desperately poor, feudal society ruled by a degenerate god-king, with a tiny, scattered, and largely illiterate population in danger of dying off from sexually transmitted diseases. Mongolians themselves speak of it as a dark time. But Mongolian pride and nationalism were simmering below the surface, and when revolution in China overthrew the Qing Dynasty in 1911, Mongolia declared its independence, with the eighth Bogd Khan as its king.

China's new leaders did not recognise Mongolia's independence but were too busy to interfere. But China still had designs on Mongolia – as did Russia, which sent 'advisors' to the newly independent land. By 1919, the Chinese had got their act together sufficiently to invade, occupy the Mongolian capital, and force the Bogd Khan to submit to their authority.

Even by the turbulent standards of Mongolian history, the twentieth century was bizarre and bloody. Mongolia was invaded again, this time by the 'Mad Baron,' Baron von Ungern-Sternberg, a volatile and probably insane White Russian general, fleeing the Bolsheviks, who hoped to establish his own Buddhist fiefdom in Mongolia. He and his ragtag private army took the Mongolian capital and set about sowing confusion and bloodshed.

By this time a small Mongolian nationalist movement had organised under the leadership of a young man named Sukhbaatar – Axe Hero. They won the support of the vacillating Bogd Khan and asked the Bolsheviks in Russia to help rid them of the Mad Baron. The Red Army obliged, and after a series of bloody battles the baron and the residual Chinese forces were sent packing. (The baron was shipped back to Russia and later executed.) On 11 July 1921, Sukhbaatar's Mongolian People's Party proclaimed a government, with the Bogd Khan – a great survivor if ever there was one – as its titular head.

Mongolia's new rulers lacked both a sophisticated ideology and the experience of power; they were in desperate need of advice on how to run a country, and they turned to the Russian revolutionaries for support. The Bolsheviks, in desperate need of allies – and, let's be charitable, in the spirit of internationalism – were happy to give it. A famous painting, which used to adorn all government offices in Mongolia (and now adorns the broom cupboards of government buildings), captures the historically approved version of the relationship: it shows a meeting between Sukhbaatar and Lenin. The young Mongolian, in a blue *del* and a gold and crimson tunic, sits in a chair and gazes into the eyes of the Russian leader. Lenin, in a sombre three-piece suit, beard jutting boldly forward, rests a hand, in fatherly support, on Sukhbaatar's forearm. His other hand is raised, index finger extended, driving home his point. From the wall above the two men, the avuncular, bearded figure of Karl Marx gazes down in approval.

The meeting almost certainly never took place, but it is a tidy scene and true in spirit. Soon the Mongolian government was following the twists and turns of the Soviet Union's political development. Within a year, the Mongolian party had undergone its first purge of 'counterrevolutionary elements.' Fourteen leaders were executed, including the country's first prime minister. In 1924, the Bogd Khan died, and no successor was named. The country was re-branded the Mongolian People's Republic and set on the path of Communism. To mark the change, the name of the country's capital was changed from Nisleel Huree – the admittedly uninspired Capital Camp – to Ulaanbaatar – Red Hero.

The history of Communist Mongolia is as convoluted and bloody, as tragic and farcical, and occasionally as heroic, as the history of the USSR. In fact, it mirrors it so closely that it's possible to employ a useful shorthand.

Sukhbaatar was Mongolia's Lenin: he led the revolution, then died at 30, reportedly of natural causes (though rumours persist that he was poisoned). His body was interred in the capital's central square –

though, unlike in Russia, you're not allowed to go and look at it.

He was followed by Choibalsan, Mongolia's Stalin: he ruled for decades, overseeing frequent and disastrous policy turns marked by famine, bloody rebellion, and regular purges of 'rightist elements.' After he died in the early 1950s, it was admitted that he had made mistakes and fostered a personality cult.

His successor, Tsedenbal, was Mongolia's Brezhnev: a dull bureaucrat but a survivor, whose seemingly endless rule was mercifully free of the excesses of his predecessor. He is thus remembered more fondly; the most common praise given to him is that he managed to keep Mongolia nominally independent of the Soviet Union, unlike the Central Asian states that were absorbed by the USSR.

Mongolia had become the world's second Communist state, but it was a country wildly unsuited to the role. It was an overwhelmingly rural land with a tiny, scattered population and not a hint of an urban proletariat. Ninety per cent of the population was illiterate, much of the nation's wealth was in the hands of a small band of nobles and an elephantine clergy, and Chinese traders controlled almost all the commerce. The process of moulding this into a socialist republic was not pretty: Choibalsan expelled the traders and expropriated the wealth of the nobles and the church – moves that were extremely unpopular. Then he embarked upon the collectivisation of livestock breeding, a scheme that attacked the independence and identity of the Mongolian nomads. Outraged herders slaughtered millions of their own animals rather than hand them over. There was famine. There were armed uprisings, a near civil war.

The authorities rethought the collectivisation policy and pulled back from the brink. They left the sturdy, independent herders more or less alone.

Livestock remained – as it remains to this day – the pillar of the economy. For everything else, Mongolia had to rely on the Soviet Union, the country's major benefactor and almost its sole trading partner, the supplier of funds and equipment and a steady stream of advisors. The USSR, in return, got access to Mongolia's raw materials and a handy buffer between it and China.

After the Second World War, in which Mongolia raised an army of 100,000 men in support of the Soviet war effort, things became more stable, and Mongolia saw some much-needed social development: the government put money into health care and education, including boarding schools for nomads' children and scholarships for bright pupils to attend Russian universities. The new Communist countries of Eastern Europe – and initially China – gave the Mongolian People's Republic broader international contacts and recognition, new sources of support. In 1961, the country was admitted to the United Nations.

The citizens of the People's Republic were better educated and healthier than any Mongolians in history. But they lost things too. They lost part of their written language when the Russians persuaded them to scrap their traditional Uighur script in favour of the Cyrillic alphabet. (This move made it easier to learn Russian but conveniently cut them off from the Mongolians of Chinese Inner Mongolia, who retained the old script.) And they lost part of their history when Chinggis Khan was written out, redrawn from a great nationalist leader to a backward feudal overlord. Educated Mongolians learned to love Pushkin and Chekhov – great writers, to be sure – and to regard their own culture as more primitive.

Mongolia remained where it had been for most of the past 700 years – trapped in a tributary of the river of history, but one the current kept turning upside down. To its Russian and Chinese neighbours, it was often an afterthought, but they played havoc with it nonetheless.

Against all odds, though, as the twentieth century wound down, the Mongolians survived as a people. Imperialism and Communism had both mounted attacks on the nomads' traditional way of life, yet it survived. It formed the bedrock of their national identity, their defining image of themselves. It's a tough life – difficult, lonely and spartan. But it has made them a stubborn lot.

Russia still called the shots, though. The Russians funded industry for the better extraction of Mongolia's natural resources, building a giant copper mine and several industrial cities on the steppe; and, as the USSR's relations with China worsened, they built up a vast, now abandoned and crumbling but still largely secret military infrastructure – army and air bases, bunkers, missile sites and a uranium mine – and shipped in 100,000 Russian troops. During the Sino-Soviet dispute, Mongolia obediently abandoned its rapprochement with China, expelling the Chinese traders and the labourers who'd constructed many of Ulaanbaatar's finest buildings.

Russia's support propped up the Mongolian economy but did not nurture it. A kinder, gentler livestock collectivisation was introduced – one that gave herders control over where to graze herds – but it did not eliminate the risky, subsistence nature of cattle herding. Harsh winters were still likely to wipe out millions of animals and throw the economy into crisis. Mongolia was still overwhelmingly dependent on Russian imports and on large infusions of Soviet aid.

And then, one day, it all disappeared. It happened quickly. First there was the loosening of control, fatigue on the part of the authorities after all those iron-grip decades; the images from Berlin and Prague and Bucharest, followed by the first tentative demonstrations in Sukhbaatar Square; the government's decision that perhaps elections were not such a bad idea, that perhaps there was a place in the government for political opponents and a place in the economy for private enterprise; an Ulaanbaatar Spring in 1990, the winds of change.

Then the Soviet Union collapsed and with it the supply of money that had amounted to 30 per cent of the country's GDP. The Russian soldiers and advisors went home. The results were fuel shortages, closed factories, unemployment, scarcity. It has been called the greatest peacetime economic collapse in history.

And Mongolia was on its own. Well, not quite on its own. The World Bank and the International Monetary Fund, the Asian Development Bank and the United

Nations, countries such as Germany, the United States and Japan – all were happy to step in with loans and grants and advice for the country's young new leaders: how to run a parliamentary democracy; how to set up a stock exchange and run a market economy; how to respect human rights and protect the environment. The Western Buddhists and Mongolists arrived, bearing pictures of the Dalai Lama and Chinggis Khan, happy to teach the Mongolians how to be Mongolians again.

And the Mongolians, in their *gers* and their Soviet-built flats with the cracks and the bad plumbing, looked around, took deep breaths, and plunged in.

Chapter Three

The Nomad and the Carpetbagger

The factory owner, tall and alien-thin, swept into his office, flung his cashmere overcoat onto a hook, and sat down, levering his stick-insect legs under his big, big desk. He folded his hands and looked at me. 'We'll never solve the world's economic problems,' he said, 'without a third world war.'

I was taken aback by this opener. Jargalsaikhan was one of Mongolia's most famous capitalists and the owner of Buyan, the country's largest private cashmere manufacturer. I'd come to discuss the troubled state of the wool industry. I'd yet to open my mouth. Momentarily at a loss, I stared past him out the window to the car park, where his black Humvee stood gleaming.

But Jargalsaikhan wasn't waiting for my questions. 'A nuclear war wouldn't be so bad for Mongolia,' he continued. 'For China, yes, but not for Mongolia. We have lots of land and not too many people.'

Jargalsaikhan was *A Character*. Mongolia likes characters, so he got plenty of ink in the newspapers. In addition to being preternaturally tall and gaunt and driving the rutted streets of Ulaanbaatar in the gargantuan Hummer, he had his own political party, the Republican Party (which failed to win a single seat in the 1996 general election). He had an opinion on everything and was a vociferous, contemptuous critic of Mongolia's Democratic Coalition government.

'The American Republican Party supports these

thieves in the government,' he was telling me now, as the interview spun out of my control. 'They are not principled men. They have little culture or education. They only care about money. There's no democracy in Mongolia because of corruption and nepotism.'

An interview with Jargalsaikhan, I discovered, quickly turned into a monologue about his pet hates (US world domination, Chinese expansionism, the government) and his idiosyncratic passions. Chief among the latter seemed to be President Clinton – to whom he had sent several cashmere items via Madeleine Albright during the US secretary of state's visit to Mongolia in 1998; he proudly showed me the letter of thanks he had received from the president's office – and himself. He informed me that he would soon be in Washington and would be dropping in on Bill Clinton for a chat. 'Imagine! The son of an ordinary nomad can meet the president of the United States and talk about politics.' He glowed with self-satisfaction.

Jargalsaikhan was one of Mongolia's new import-export elite. He liked to tell the story of how he'd started out by selling Chinese jeans in Ulaanbaatar's markets, though he tended to skimp on the details of how he'd been transformed, within a decade, from market trader to cashmere baron. His story was typical: almost all of Mongolia's new business barons make their money in 'import-export' (the export of raw materials and the import of consumer goods) rather than in manufacturing.

There's precious little manufacturing in Mongolia these days. Soviet money, Soviet fuel and Soviet parts built the country's factories and kept them running; now basic goods that were made in the country until a few years ago, simple things such as matches, must be imported. In 1997, as part of its economic liberalisation policy, the government removed all import duties. The result was a flood of hitherto unavailable luxuries.

I was surprised at how much *stuff* you could buy in Ulaanbaatar's shops (for what, by Western standards, were extremely reasonable prices): a Mercedes or a four-wheel drive, a colour TV or electric ice-cream maker, a top-of-the-line laptop or a bottle of expensive French wine.

Clearly this was all to the good. Clearly, too, there was a widening chasm between the small elite that could afford to buy these luxury items and the majority, who stared through the plate-glass windows of the Sony showroom on Ulaanbaatar's main drag, Peace Avenue, in wonder.

All of the new businessmen I met (and they were almost always men) in Ulaanbaatar's beer bars and offices and conference rooms were, like Jargalsaikhan, bullish and self-confident. They never spoke about the thing that baffled me most – where their start-up capital came from. I don't know. I do know that, for most of the 1990s, Mongolia's fledgling commercial banking system was in a state of chaos. Several banks collapsed under the weight of bad loans. A number of bank executives were jailed. In 1998, the government-owned Reconstruction Bank was declared insolvent; millions of dollars in loans it had given were unaccounted for. I also know that of US$190 million in foreign grants and loans received by Mongolia between 1991 and 1996, $15 million was found – by the government's own audit committee – to have been 'improperly used.' Another $11 million in loans was never repaid; millions of dollars more was simply missing.

I toyed with these thoughts as Jargalsaikhan gave me the approved version of his life story.

'I started out by selling copper scrap to Hong Kong,' he said. 'Then I sold Chinese clothes and electronics in Russia and in Mongolia. I was testing out what sectors were profitable. Copper and gold have 5 to 10 per cent profit margins. With cashmere, it's 50 per cent. Also, it's an established business, and Mongolia has a lot of raw materials. So I started a cashmere factory.'

Cashmere, the downy-soft wool produced by goats, was a cushion for Mongolia's economy in a tumultuous decade. The country produces almost a third of the world's cashmere and is the second-largest global supplier of the wool, after China. Ulaanbaatar-based Gobi Cashmere, still one of the world's largest cashmere producers, was one of the few state-owned firms to weather the first difficult years of transition.

As Mongolia opened up, many aspiring businesspeople saw cashmere as one of the country's key exports. In 1993, Gobi was one of three cashmere exporters in Mongolia. By 1999, there were 20, most exporting raw or semiprocessed wool to China, Europe or Japan.

Good old goat down provided a steady supply of export income for the struggling country – and for the hundreds of thousands of herding families hurled into the market economy. In 1990, less than a third of Mongolia's livestock was in private hands; today, nearly all of it is. Herders, given the chance to make decisions and own livestock, opted for goats in a big way; between 1990 and 1999, the country's goat population doubled, to 11 million.

Herders could sell the valuable wool to traders who toured the countryside or gathered in town markets. Or they could trade directly for durable goods: motorbikes, television sets, even trucks. More often, the modest cash income from cashmere allowed herders to buy a few items of store-bought food or clothing to supplement their subsistence lives.

Among the capitalists, Jargalsaikhan stood out in realising that there was more money to be made selling finished garments than exporting wool alone. He also saw that it was possible to make sweaters in styles someone other than your grandmother might wear. Soon he was exporting his company's stylish sweaters and scarves to Europe and Japan.

But it seemed, by 1998 or 1999, that the modest good times might be over. Mongolia's economy depends largely on exporting raw materials, particularly copper, cashmere and gold. When the Asian economic crisis struck, prices for all three took a dive.

Suddenly the demand for luxury sweaters declined. By early 1999, a kilogram of Mongolian cashmere that had been processed to remove unwanted dirt and coarse hairs was selling for US$40. Two or three years earlier, it had fetched up to $120. So, while the country was selling more of the wool than ever before, it was getting less and less for it.

This is the problem with Mongolia's resource-based economy; it is easily buffeted by forces beyond its control.

When Soviet subsidies and support were withdrawn in the early 1990s, Mongolia's economy went into a tailspin. The flow of fuel, spare parts and Russian technicians dried up; factories closed.

The neoliberal policies introduced by the government from 1996 on initially seemed to produce results: inflation dropped, the currency stabilised and trade increased. But during my time in Mongolia, imports far outstripped exports, and the government posted alarming revenue shortfalls. By 1999, transfer payments to local governments had become sporadic, and teachers, pensioners and civil servants were going unpaid for months at a time.

What did the government do? It sold off chunks of its hard-currency reserves, it asked for more foreign aid, and it tried to generate money from taxes.

This last strategy has not been a success. Mongolians do not like paying taxes – who does? – and the novice democratic government lacked the authority, and the resources, to force them to do it. In mid-1997, in an arguably sensible move to bolster domestic cashmere producers, the government imposed a tax on exports of raw cashmere. This tax led to one of the most striking statistics I have ever seen: reported cashmere exports fell by more than 98 per cent, from more than US$16 million in 1997 to a little over $300,000 in 1998. The rest, it's fair to assume, was smuggled out across Mongolia's long, sparsely defended border with China.

Even the quality of Mongolian cashmere was under threat. The president of the country's Wool and Cashmere Federation told me, a little ruefully, that Mongolian cashmere was generally considered the second best in the world. The best? China's. She said the collapse of breeding programmes and other forms of agricultural support – and a 'quantity over quality' mentality – had led to substandard goats infiltrating herds. And most Mongolian companies, even those with foreign investment, lacked the technology to make finished cashmere goods in the country. It's a vicious cycle: there is no money for investment in infrastructure and technology, so quality deteriorates, and prices fall.

Like most of Mongolia's remaining manufacturing businesses, the Wool and Cashmere Federation was not a fan of the tax holiday on imports – especially as goods exported to neighbouring China and Russia were taxed by those countries.

I raised all these issues with Jargalsaikhan, who looked supremely unconcerned. As an exporter largely of finished garments, he was insulated from the worst of the price fall, which he said would hit wool suppliers and retailers much harder than it hit him. And in some ways the Asian crisis had been good for Mongolia. The cost of Korean cars had gone down, leading to a proliferation of Daewoos and Kias on Ulaanbaatar's streets.

Jargalsaikhan knew what this country needed (and he'd tell me for free): tough love. 'Over the last seven years, the ADB, the IMF, various governments have given Mongolia too much in loans and foreign aid,' he said. 'How can we survive if we get used to this? We should have been using these loans to improve our lives and create jobs. But we just ate them. This had to happen. Sooner or later, we had to reach this point. But in a way it's good. When someone is hungry, he will work harder.'

It wasn't far, maybe 50 miles, from Jargalsaikhan's IKEA-styled office to the *ger* of herder Baatar, but it was all the way down the cashmere food chain. Baatar, who'd pitched his tent in the shelter of a hillside in the grasslands east of the capital, was a typical small herder: he kept a few horses, some cows, a few dozen sheep and about 30 goats.

He was happy to have the money he gained from selling his goats' wool at the open-air raw-materials market in Ulaanbaatar, but he had little idea of what was done with it and less control over the price he was paid.

'We comb the goats once a year, in the spring,' he explained, showing me a fierce-looking, long-toothed metal comb that was used to rake through the hair of a trussed and protesting goat, lifting out the fine down beneath.

'We sell the wool to a trading company, which sells it on. I don't really know what they do with it or what's the final destination. I comb about five kilos a year from my goats, and I used to get quite a bit of money, 14,000 to 17,000 tugrug for a kilo. Now I hear it's down to

7,000 or 8,000. But I'll still sell it. Some people hang on to theirs to see if the price will go up, but not me. What am I going to do with raw cashmere?'

Not, perhaps, the entrepreneurial spirit the government would like to hear. Baatar did not see his goats as four-legged money machines; his relationship with them was more direct.

He reached out a hand to stroke a four-day-old kid, one of a trio that had been let inside to keep warm by the *ger*'s soot-blackened iron stove. 'I mostly have black and red goats,' he said, 'as well as a few whites. The blacks and the reds give the best cashmere, but the whites give the best meat.

'The thing with sheep and goats is, they are pretty adaptable animals. We feed the kids, but we don't have to worry about the older ones. They can dig through the snow in winter, unlike cows, which can't feed themselves in heavy snow.

'I'd say the goat is the most valuable animal you can have, because it's the most productive. We can sell the cashmere, and we can make yogurt and butter from the milk. Goat's milk is lovely – it's the most rich and delicious dairy product there is.

'Anyway,' he said, 'I'm not a real expert in goats. You should talk to my neighbour Sukhbaatar. He's a clever one.'

Sukhbaatar lived about half a mile away, a courteous man in his fifties or sixties (it's so hard to tell with Mongolians) who lived with his wife in one of two *gers* set beside a tidy paddock. He had about 20 cashmere goats – though he kept insisting that he wasn't a 'real herder.' By this he meant that, like thousands of other Mongolians of his generation, he had spent most of his working life in the city but had gone back to the land when the economic crisis struck.

Sukhbaatar had grown up in a herding family, but like all herders' children under Communism, he'd been sent away to boarding school and had ended up a teacher and party worker in Nalaikh, a busy coal-mining town. Now the mine was closed, and his pension was not nearly enough to live on in the city.

'It's quite a common story nowadays,' he said, as we sat around the stove in his *ger*. 'My wife and I decided it would be better to use the money we'd saved during our working lives to buy some animals. It's not a bad life, because we have some animals that can supply our needs. They give us meat and milk.

'We do get some money from selling our cashmere, but mostly we prefer this life because it's just easier. At Tsagaan Sar, the lunar New Year holiday, I didn't have to worry about how I was going to scrape together the money to buy a sheep for the celebrations – I just slaughtered one of my herd.'

His wife, who'd been working away briskly at the stove, placed a steaming tray of mutton dumplings on the table in front of us. Another one of the herd.

'I'm not a real herder,' Sukhbaatar said again. 'I'm just trying to survive. So I follow my herd.'

Chapter Four

Back to the Future

Two red-cheeked girls on horseback were thundering at us across the desert, laughing. A stream of horses flowed along in their wake. The pair slowed to a trot as they reached their patch of stony gravel in the ocean of stony gravel that is the Gobi, their homestead, with its wisps of midsummer grass, its nearby well, its *ger* battened down with ropes tied to rocks against the unrelenting desert wind.

They jumped down, tied their mounts to a thin rope that stretched like a clothesline between two posts and left the other horses to wander. A clump of camel calves sprawled in the shelter of the *ger*, mewling.

'Oh, hello,' said the girls, still breathless and giggling. 'Excuse us. We were just rounding up the horses.'

The horses stayed close to the *ger*. The wind really was fierce, whipping the animals' tails and manes into gestures of alarm, pelting us with fine grains of sand. The two girls – sisters, I could see – wore sturdy leather boots, dusty *dels*, and scarves on their heads to keep off the sun.

'We stopped,' I said, 'because we were curious about *that*.' I pointed just to the left of the *ger* at a concave silver dish, with a small mast in the middle, poking up at the blue desert sky.

'You mean the satellite dish?' said the younger, plumper, more effusive girl as her sister looked away and giggled into her hand. 'Oh, it's great. We get 16 or

17 channels – CNN and everything. My favourite is Star Sports – I love to watch the motorbike racing.'

She said her name was Surenjav. She was 19, and her sister, Byambajav, was 22. They lived in the *ger* with their parents. They were nomads, moving their *ger* twice a year to summer and winter pastures. They'd also make frequent shorter moves in summer to find fresh grass for the animals; the cover in the desert was so sparse the livestock would chew it clean. It didn't take long to dismantle a *ger*; it could be done in an hour.

In addition to the dish, there was a battered red Russian Planeta motorbike sitting in the shade of the tent – a sign of wealth among herders, a lifeline of mobility in the desert.

'Do you want to see?' asked Surenjav. She took us over to the dish. In black letters on its shiny surface was the name of the company that supplied it: Malchin – herders. On the other side of the *ger*, a wind turbine whirled.

'We bought it about four years ago from a trader who travels around the area,' Surenjav explained. 'It was 800,000 tugrug for the whole package: the dish, the wind generator and a colour television.'

Almost six hundred pounds. Big money.

'It's really good, because you can learn about the outside world, see how other people live. This life can be a bit lonely. The nearest neighbour is half a mile away, and it's 45 miles to Dalanzadgad, the provincial capital.'

It was odd; that was the first time I'd heard a Mongolian speak of loneliness. I'd always thought herding must be a terribly solitary life.

'Well, we weren't always herders, you know,' said Surenjav, with a hint of pride. 'We used to live in the city. I've been to high school!'

'In Ulaanbaatar?' I asked.

'No – in Choir. I miss that life sometimes.'

Choir was a desolate desert town on the Trans-Mongolian rail line, a former Soviet military base, where people lived in the hulks of Russian army buildings or in *gers* pitched amid the rubble. It was one of the grimmest places I'd ever seen.

'Why did you leave?' I asked.

'The economy in the city is not so good. My mother will be home soon. She can tell you all about it. Come inside.'

She led us inside the *ger*, sat us down around the stove. Byambajav prepared a pot of salty milk tea in silence, but Surenjav was keen to chat to strangers.

'We subscribe to four newspapers,' she said proudly. 'And sometimes we take the motorbike to Dalanzadgad to buy books and magazines.

'Don't misunderstand me. This is a good life. We've done well – we have more than 500 animals. It's a better life than in the city, because we don't have to worry about food, and we can make some money from selling animals, sheepskins, cashmere and camel wool.

'But it's a hard life. We sleep for six hours, and the rest of the time it's all work. We have to get up at sunrise to milk the camels and water the animals; then we take the herds out to pasture, and later we bring them in again. Sometimes we miss our city life, especially when the weather is bad. It's a more interesting life, because you have your friends. Here your neighbours are so far away.'

Did she have any friends her own age?

'There aren't too many young people around. But I have a boyfriend,' she said, turning ever so slightly redder.

'What does he do?' I asked.

'He's a herder.' Duh. 'He lives 20 miles away. We see each other once a week. He'll come over here and watch TV, or sometimes I go to his *ger*. He has a TV as well.'

The door's spring hinges gave a creak, and a woman in her forties entered. She was dressed in a clean maroon *del*, a compact, tidy woman with smooth, sandblasted skin, neatly cropped black hair, and silver earrings glinting above fine, high cheekbones. Surenjav told her, in a rush, who we were, why we'd stopped. She went to the stove, refilled our bowls of tea, then perched on the edge of a bed and looked at us levelly. Her movements were neat, efficient, authoritative. Her name, she said, was Odmaa.

'I was born in this country, the Gobi,' she said, 'but after school I trained to become a doctor, and I went to work in the city. I lived there for 15 years. I worked in the hospital, and my husband was a driver, and we raised a family. But I missed my home country.

'When the transition came,' she continued, using the word, *transition*, that Mongolians and development workers alike always employed to refer to the decade after the collapse of Communism – a word so much more orderly and reasonable than revolution, or cataclysm, or any of the others I could think of. 'When the transition came, it became a lot easier to move around. You could go where you liked.

'And, at the same time, life in the city became much harder. The factories closed, the price of everything went up – even if you had a job, it was hard to survive. So we decided to come back here and teach our children how to raise animals. From an economic standpoint, it's much easier to have animals than to live in town. My colleagues in the city earn $40 a month. If you have to buy your meat and milk from the market, you can't live on that.'

Thousands of other Mongolian families had done the same thing. They had gone back to their roots, back to the land. Amid the economic chaos of the 1990s, livestock were the one stable thing in a world turned upside down. Animals were wealth and life itself – they were meat and milk and money.

As the twentieth century ended, Mongolia was one of the few countries in the world experiencing mass migration from the city to the country. For many, rural life was an existence just as precarious as remaining in the city would have been. Odmaa had grown up herding, but many of the city-raised Mongolians going back to the land hadn't the faintest idea how to begin, how to find rich pasture in summer and a sheltered camp in winter. One unusually harsh winter could wipe out a whole herd.

I didn't worry for Odmaa, though. She was in control, capable, I could tell. But I thought I could detect a hint, just the slightest ripple, of wistfulness in her voice.

'Our standard of living has improved here,' she said

in a measured, decisive, tone. 'I want my children to be herders, because even if you have a university degree these days the pay is not so high. But maybe for my grandchildren it would be better to get some education and live in town. Now we are working to give our grandchildren opportunities. My children have animals – they have assets.'

We thanked her for the tea and got up to go. Surenjav showed us to the door and followed us out to the jeep.

'My mother thinks it's a shame that we lost our close ties with Russia,' she said. 'My parents firmly believe that the socialist time was much better than this. They remember it fondly. They say things like, "All for one, and one for all." Now you have to rely completely on yourself.'

Chapter Five

The School for Scandal

To the few foreign observers who paid attention, Mongolia's 1996 general election seemed to be an inspiring example of democracy at work. The young dissidents whose brave demonstrations in a freezing Sukhbaatar Square in 1990 had cracked the ice of the Communist regime appeared to have reached political maturity. They had formed political parties and – learning the lesson of 1992, when a fragmented opposition had returned a Communist majority government – united under the banner of the Democratic Coalition.

On polling day, 30 June, the small press corps who'd flown in for the event was rewarded with a tidy, dramatic and eye-catching story: a voter turnout of more than 90 per cent, images of grizzled nomads riding miles across the steppe to cast their ballots, and a resounding vote for change. The Democrats, running on a platform of economic liberalisation, individual freedom and sweeping privatisation, won 50 seats in the 76-seat parliament. The (now ex-) Communists of the Mongolian People's Revolutionary Party took only 25.

There was jubilation – especially in the camp of the foreign diplomats and advisors in Ulaanbaatar who had done so much to craft the outlook of the country's young new rulers. It was, everyone agreed, the dawn of a new era, in which Mongolia would look neither north to Russia nor south to China but outward, and mostly west, to the World Bank, the IMF and the United States.

One of the enduring media myths of the election is the Mongolians' love of Newt Gingrich, the hard-right speaker of the US Congress and the genius behind the 1994 Contract with Americans. The Mongolian Democrats – advised by a helpful delegation from the International Republican Institute – had published and publicised their own US-inspired election manifesto, the Contract with Voters. More than one foreign media report featured gnarled herders in their *gers* professing a deep admiration for the American legislator.

Well, it's a nice story. I'd have used it too. But let's be prudent and say that most Mongolians greeted the election results with cautious optimism. They had voted for the Democrats out of a mixture of nationalism, fatigue at cronyism and corruption, and a simple desire for change. Some old-timers doubted the wisdom of the new government's neoliberal economic policies or suspected that the Democrats might have a hard time delivering on their promises of prosperity – especially the privatisation of land, which ran counter to the whole structure of nomadic life, a structure far older than Communism. But hopes were high.

By the time I arrived in Mongolia a year later, the Democrats were coming apart at the seams. And they had a lot of seams.

Mongolians are fast learners. In the autumn of 1997, in parliament and on the streets, Mongolian democracy seems loud, combative and vibrant. In the legislature, the State Ikh Hural – literally the 'Great Meeting' – the opposition declaims and denounces. The government sputters and defends. Outside, pensioners complain about the meagreness of their pensions, and students protest, as students do, for lower fees. The Communists call for votes of no-confidence, votes that the Democrats, with their huge majority, easily survive.

'The government is ignoring the public interest to fulfil their own ambitions,' intones the opposition's crafty and articulate leader, Enkhbayar. 'They are making a mockery of democracy.' Despite his party's utter lack of experience of democracy, he says it with absolute conviction.

'The MPRP is blaming the government for the mistakes of the last seventy years,' replies Enkhsaikhan, the plump and smiling young prime minister, with all the confidence of one who has the world's opinion behind him. It is a fine performance all around.

Outside, in nearby Freedom – formerly Lenin – Square, a more or less permanent anti-government demonstration has grown up, organised by a handful of small groups fond of suspiciously long hunger strikes and unwieldy names: the Mongolian United Movement, the Union for Social Security and Honesty. The protesters consist largely of stooped pensioners with threadbare robes and chests full of medals, complaining about skyrocketing prices, plummeting pensions and disappearing health care, old people who use words such as *betrayal*.

The government doesn't seem to be too bothered by them. As 1998 dawns, the Democrats announce that in the coming year they will increase the pace of reform: they will stabilise the economy while speeding up privatisation; they will improve the country's

THE SCHOOL FOR SCANDAL

infrastructure and social services while spending less money.

The international advisors applaud. Plucky little Mongolia is definitely on-message.

But not everyone is convinced. In early spring, calls for the government's resignation begin to surface again. Only this time they are coming not from the opposition but from within the Democrats' own camp. The instigator is an MP named Elbegdorj, a squat 35-year-old former journalist with a ready smile and a sweaty brow. His argument is this: the reason for the government's plummeting popularity is a 'lack of coordination' between parliament and cabinet, which is formed, in the American manner, of extraparliamentary appointees. If the government were made up of members of parliament, the problem would be solved. As the Democrats' parliamentary leader, Elbegdorj would be the new prime minister.

Enkhsaikhan objects in the strongest possible terms, and the Democrats set to fighting among themselves: the Elbegdorj faction against the Enkhsaikhan faction. Possibly there is real frustration behind the scrap, a genuine desire to govern well. But to most observers, it looks like a naked power struggle: less than two years after being thrust from obscurity to office, Elbegdorj and other MPs long for a level of power, prestige and perks they can't attain as mere backbenchers.

Mongolians of my acquaintance look pained. 'It's a disgrace,' says a colleague. 'It's because we have little experience of democracy.'

'Actually,' I say, trying to cheer her up, 'this sort of thing goes on all the time in Western countries.'

She looks at me with frank disbelief. I can tell she thinks I am just being polite.

On 20 April, Enkhsaikhan presents his resignation to parliament after the governing bodies of both Democratic Coalition parties – the National Democrats and the Social Democrats – vote for his ouster. It is accepted with only one dissenting vote.

'I believe history will show that there were more achievements than mistakes while this government was in office,' says the fallen PM in a televised farewell address.

Three days later, Elbegdorj is handed the seal of office. The new prime minister names a new cabinet composed of relatively unknown and inexperienced MPs.

The Democrats' unity is crumbling. Some Social Democrats begin to speak openly of dissolving the coalition and uniting with the MPRP.

Outside, the protests continue. Three of the demonstrators keeping up the anti-government vigil announce they will immolate themselves on 1 May – May Day – unless the entire parliament resigns. The Mongolian Lawyers Association turns down their request for legal aid.

On 29 April, parliament votes on the new cabinet. Four of the nine nominees are rejected. Several of the candidates, notes the MPRP drily, fail 'to meet the professional and moral standards required by the top government positions.'

On the last day of April, the protesters meet with the

speaker of parliament and agree to call off the self-immolation after he agrees to conduct a nationwide referendum on the government's performance. 'Parliament can't resign just because someone threatens to set himself alight,' notes one Democrat MP.

Amid all this, on 2 May, US Secretary of State Madeleine Albright pays a goodwill visit to Mongolia. It is a moment of triumph for the Democrats – like a royal seal of approval – undercut by their embarrassing disarray. Albright jets in, stays for seven hours, and bestows her benediction. 'Mongolia,' she says, 'is independent and peaceful, proud and free. The United States wants Mongolia to succeed.' It is as much a command as a commendation.

On a carefully managed visit to a herding family on Ulaanbaatar's rural fringe, Albright is presented with her own horse. Alas, she has to leave it behind.

Post-Albright, the Democrats continue to struggle to get their act together. On 6 May, MPs vote on four new candidates to fill the vacant cabinet posts. Two are rejected. One of those approved is Zorig, bespectacled student leader turned respected MP, who is put in charge of infrastructure.

On 8 May, the prime minister dredges up two new cabinet nominees from his dwindling list of eligible MPs. The legislators are invited to ask questions of the candidates. None does. When it comes to the vote, both are rejected.

The next day, the Democrats suffer another blow when one of their MPs is killed in a paragliding accident. It has become a popular sport among a group of young political high-flyers, who on weekends can be seen floating down from the mountains that surround the city.

Meanwhile, the government's vaunted promises of reform are stalling. The head of the State Property Committee admits that, of the 1,114 entities slated for privatisation, only a third have been sold off.

On 19 May, drivers in Ulaanbaatar confront an almost unheard-of event: a traffic jam. Anti-government protesters block a central intersection for four hours to back their demand for the resignation of parliament and the prosecution of corrupt MPs. The city's bus company says it will sue for losses.

The Democrats try again on 21 May to fill the two remaining cabinet posts. One of their nominees is approved. The other is rejected – the fourth candidate for the post of minister of education who does not make the grade.

A week later, it's fifth time lucky. The education portfolio is filled by a 28-year-old MP named Saikhanbileg by a margin of one vote. The government's relief is short-lived. The same day, a motion is read out in parliament calling on the entire Hural to resign. It is signed by four MPs, including one from the Democratic Coalition. 'We must be ready to sacrifice ourselves to save our country from the tragedy of extinction,' it says ominously.

By the start of June, the government has become a joke to Mongolians. But at least the cabinet is complete. Then the opposition walks out of parliament. The government has ordered the merger of a failing state-owned bank with a private institution. By the government's own admission, 70 per cent of the Reconstruction Bank's US$13.7 million in outstanding loans is 'unreliable' – which everyone understands to mean unrecoverable. The bank, set up by the government only 18 months earlier, was ordered to stop lending in February but carried on oblivious, handing out $9 million in three months.

The MPRP is livid. Enkhbayar calls the merger 'a conspiracy' to put public money into private hands – the hands of the government and its friends. One of the directors of the private bank that stands to absorb the Reconstruction Bank is a prominent Democrat MP. In the weeks that follow, several more MPs, their families, and their businesses are linked by the opposition and the press to loans from the bank.

The government argues that it is acting to disentangle the wreckage of a banking system it inherited from the previous regime. The merger, it points out, has the approval of the World Bank and the IMF. But the Communists know they are on to a winner here. Most Mongolians have noted the suspiciously high proportion of Mercedes drivers and Italian-suit wearers among MPs, who earn the equivalent of less than £70 a month. They have read of the businesses registered to brothers and husbands and wives, of the children sent to university in the United States or Britain. The bank merger gives focus to their resentment and envy and discontent.

The furor gains intensity. Radio and television broadcast live from parliament as MPs hurl shouts and accusations. The president warns that, if 'urgent measures' are not taken, he will dissolve parliament. Worse, an all-party task force set up to investigate the merger rules that the government has indeed broken the law.

Elbegdorj continues to smile, but he sees the writing on the wall. He tells a group of foreign reporters that, 'Even if the government resigns or there is a new election, it will not mean that Mongolia will reverse its chosen path. The people have already made their choice.'

The demonstrations, given a focus at last, grow louder. The opposition continues its boycott, and parliament scuds to a standstill.

The timing is particularly unfortunate. At the end of June, the World Bank sponsors a conference designed to lure foreign companies to invest in Mongolia. It is a tough sell. The government is paralysed, the country's resource-dependent export income is plummeting, and the banking system is shaky. The Democrats do their stoic best. 'We Mongolians will change the perception that it is hard to invest in Mongolia,' Elbegdorj tells his audience of potential investors in the conference room of the Chinggis Khan Hotel. Government pitchmen do their best to talk up the country: it's 'the gateway to China,' 'the gateway to Russia,' even – bizarrely and a bit desperately – 'the gateway to Kazakhstan.' World Bank reps flit about wearing tight smiles. The auditorium is full, but 650 of the 800 participants are Mongolian businesspeople with hungry looks. At an outdoor reception at the government's private valley estate, one of them faces facts. 'We're all looking for foreign investors, but everybody here is Mongolian,' he says with exasperation.

A week after the conference, the government reluctantly admits that a grand total of three projects have been signed as a result of the event.

As July goes on, parliament remains deadlocked – but the government continues to make decisions. It decides to license a casino in Ulaanbaatar as a revenue-generating measure. It awards the contract to a firm partly backed by businessmen from the gambling enclave of Macau. The move surprises many people because another firm, with German investment, has been operating a casino in the Chinggis Khan Hotel for two years. Several Democrat MPs have been among its most regular customers. Now it is told to pack up and leave.

Some Democrat MPs are beginning to waver on the bank merger. 'To agree to a compromise and to retreat are the beginning of victory,' one tells parliament.

On 10 July, after six weeks, the government finally backs down. It announces that the new bank formed by the merger will be 'predominantly state-owned.' But the opposition smells blood. The police begin criminal investigations into the minister of finance and the governor of the Bank of Mongolia.

It is an exceptionally hot summer. On 21 July, eight student demonstrators go on a hunger strike in a bid to force the government to resign. They last 12 days, consuming only a litre of water a day. They give up after the prime minister promises to pay more attention to social problems.

On 24 July, parliament holds a vote of no-confidence in the Elbegdorj government. It is the first time opposition MPs have taken their seats in nearly two months. The government loses by a vote of 42 to 33. Fifteen Democrat MPs have voted with the opposition to bring down the government.

Three months after Elbegdorj engineered his ascent to office, the Democrats have the chance to form their third government in two years. Enkhbayar, the MPRP leader, reminds them that he will support a new government only if it repeals the bank merger. 'The government,' he charges, 'is deeply enmeshed in a web of corruption and official crime.'

Amid all this, the minister of finance announces that Mongolia's deficit has grown by US$70 million in the past year, while government revenues are far short of the target.

On 13 August, the Democrats nominate their new prime minister, a prominent MP named Ganbold. This time President Bagabandi, a diminutive MPRP supporter with a pencil-thin moustache like a 1920s villain, rejects him, arguing that Ganbold must take partial responsibility for the disastrous bank merger. The Democrats accuse the president of overstepping his constitutional authority. They say it is for parliament, not the president, to decide. Constitutional experts are consulted. They waver. It seems that Mongolia's spanking-new constitution, drawn up in seven heady weeks in 1991–92, is an ambiguous document.

While the debate rages inside the State Ikh Hural, outside in Freedom Square a disabled man named Jambal douses himself with petrol and sets himself ablaze. He suffers burns to his legs before police put out the flames. He tells reporters that he, his wife and three children – all deaf – live on a pension equivalent to less than £6 a month.

The next day, parliament votes to scrap the bank merger. The debacle is later estimated to have cost – depending on whom you believe – between US$4 million and $17 million. The Democrats try once again to nominate Ganbold for prime minister. Again the president rejects him. In the next two weeks, Bagabandi will reject Ganbold a total of six times. The president counters by suggesting his own candidate, another Democrat MP whose name, confusingly enough, is also Ganbold. Both sides continue to cite the constitution in support of their claims.

The institutions of democratic government, seemingly solid as granite, are as friable and fragile as sand. Without roots in Mongolia, they are swirling away like a dust storm in the desert. And Mongolians are passing from political optimism to cynicism with alarming speed. 'They're doing this on purpose, you know,' a man says to me at the bus stop one day. 'They're dragging it out so they can keep their posts for a little longer and fulfil their unfinished plans.' People around us nod in agreement.

On 2 September, parliament finally gets to vote on a new prime minister. The president and the Democrats have agreed on the nomination of Amarjargal,

Elbegdorj's 37-year-old foreign minister. He has studied in Britain, speaks English well, and is regarded as affable and competent. Yet Amarjargal is rejected by a vote of 36-35. In a gentlemanly move, he did not vote on his own nomination. A faction of Democrat MPs, now openly hostile to the Elbegdorj majority, has shot down the candidate.

The Democrats' third nominee for prime minister is rejected as unsuitable because he sports a pair of drunk-driving charges. A fourth is also summarily dispatched by the president. Two months after he resigned, Elbegdorj remains the acting prime minister. The coalition, crows Enkhbayar of the MPRP, is 'insulting the Mongolian nation and its laws.'

In September, winter begins to toy with Mongolia. In October, it settles in for a long stay. The snow comes, the cold hardens to an even, icy chill. On October 2, a Friday, Zorig, the acting infrastructure minister, stays late at the office. He does some work and plays chess. Around 10 p.m., he phones his wife to say he is heading home. When he arrives at his flat, he is stabbed 16 times by two masked intruders. He dies on the spot.

The next day, there is palpable shock, like the silence after a gasp. Zorig was quieter than many of his Democrat colleagues, and the more respected for it: chess-mad, bespectacled, plump, in contrast to the skinny young university lecturer who, a decade earlier, had stood in Sukhbaatar Square and helped to change the course of Mongolian history.

His wife, who tells police she was bound and locked in the bathroom while the murderers waited for her husband to return, reports several items missing from the flat: two gold rings, a pair of earrings, five silver bowls, the equivalent of more than £200 in cash – and, bizarrely, bottles of soy sauce and vinegar. The police suggest Zorig may have been killed by robbers.

No one believes it. The death is too symbolic. Both the Democrats and the opposition release statements denouncing the murder as an attack on Mongolia's democracy. The president goes on radio and television to appeal for calm.

But it isn't anger I sense on the unusually quiet streets of Ulaanbaatar. It is sorrow – and disgust. No one knows for sure whom to blame. As infrastructure minister, Zorig oversaw the big-money deals: the casinos and the mines. The Russian mafia? Macau gangsters? 'It's a political plot by the president,' says one man. 'It's his rivals in the coalition – he was the only one left who could be prime minister,' avers another. But deep down they all agree. It was the state of the nation that killed Zorig. He died for Mongolia's sins.

All weekend, hundreds of people hold candlelight vigils in front of Government House. On Monday, when Zorig's body lies in state, thousands queue up to pay their respects. In the thin, clear light of dawn, the line snakes across the vastness of Sukhbaatar Square. The ground is covered in globs of dried wax. Many people carry *khadags*, swatches of blue silk. Others weep, silently; it's a shock to me to see Mongolians cry.

'This was an attack on democracy,' says one young student in a fierce undertone. 'But democracy in Mongolia will only grow and get stronger.'

We wait for hours for our moment to file past the coffin, in which Zorig lies, pale and puffy, beneath a Mongolian flag.

Afterwards, people line the long route out to the dusty hilltop cemetery reserved for national heroes as Zorig's body is borne away for burial. A garish stone bust is already in place at the head of the open grave (how did they get it done so fast? I wonder, inappropriately). As the crowd mills in, I see Elbegdorj alone for a moment beside the grave; he reaches out an arm and leans on the statue for support, his eyes downcast.

It emerges that Zorig was to have been nominated for prime minister on this Monday. The president had agreed to support his candidacy. His death does not bring Mongolia's warring political factions closer together. The Democrats nominate Ganbold again. Bagabandi turns him down. For the seventh time.

After Zorig's death, everything seemed darker and more disheartening. Despite a massive police investigation, no one was ever charged with the killing. As the nights lengthened toward year's end, the political crisis continued – a theatre of the absurd, thought many, a grotesque carnival of democracy.

Democrats and Communists, government and president, continued to snipe at one another. The Democratic Coalition itself flailed in a river of torpor, swept along on a current of bitterness punctuated by eddies of violence. In October, a Democrat MP hostile to the party leadership turned up in hospital with head injuries after a bar brawl. His attacker, he said, was the head of the Democratic Union, the organisation founded a decade earlier to fight for democratic reform. He claimed his erstwhile colleagues had called him a traitor to Mongolia.

By December, the constitutional crisis had deepened. The supreme court ruled that, after all, members of parliament could not serve in government. An exhausted parliament finally appointed a prime minister. Elbegdorj, whose government had carried on for four and a half months after it resigned, finally handed over the seal of office to the appropriately low-key mayor of Ulaanbaatar, Narantsatsralt, a soft-spoken man with a hangdog look.

He didn't have many reasons to be cheerful. Mongolia was in a mess. By year's end, the government's spending outstripped its revenue by more than US$130 million. The government depended on exports of its resources – primarily copper, cashmere and gold – for desperately-needed hard currency. But now the Asian economic crisis had hit Mongolia, and prices for all three had plummeted. The Erdenet copper mine – for decades the country's primary exporter, biggest revenue generator and chief taxpayer – was tangled in a web of mismanagement, corruption and debt.

The country's filthy, crumbling power stations, the bedrock of life for Mongolia's city dwellers, were on the verge of shutting down. Increasing numbers of their customers could not pay their heat and electricity bills; the stations, in turn, could not pay the mines for the coal to stoke their huge ovens.

Even the small-scale attempts to revive wheat

production had failed. Shortages of parts and petrol meant that much of the crop remained unharvested when the first snow fell in October and had to be written off.

Mongolia's normally quiescent unions began to fill the city squares with protesters. They demanded increases in pensions and civil-service salaries and a minimum wage of 20,000 tugrug, just £14, a month. And they tapped a growing backlash against privatisation, which people were increasingly inclined to see as theft. The unions demanded the revenue from privatisation be put into social services and reviving the nation's all-but-destroyed domestic industry.

Teachers, pensioners, and civil servants were being paid sporadically, if at all – sometimes not for months on end. The problem was worst in the countryside, where there had already been a number of localised strikes and demonstrations. Because they took place in the countryside, they were completely ignored by the city elite.

Amid the crisis, the country's elected officials continued their sullen ways. It took Narantsatsralt more than a month and many votes to have his cabinet approved by parliament.

It was just another winter in Mongolia. Nothing should work – on paper, nothing does work – but life and commerce went on. Buying and selling, raising and slaughtering animals, importing and exporting, patching and mending – thriving for a few, surviving for most.

One bitter day, the sort of day when the coal dust sparkles in the sunlight and stings the back of your throat, I hauled my shopping bags from the market to the curb and stuck out my arm. A rattletrap Lada pulled up. The driver was young and burly, *del* caked in muttony dust, porkpie hat at a rakish angle. He wrenched at the rear door handle until the door popped open. I tumbled onto the carpeted back seat. We lurched off.

At a stoplight, he twisted around to have a look at me – no rearview mirror.

'Where do you come from?' he asked. 'How long have you been in Mongolia?'

I told him.

'Do you hate it here?'

'No!' I protested. 'It's very nice.'

He turned back to the road, shaking his head. 'It's bad,' he said sorrowfully. 'Like this car. Bad. Old.'

The light changed. He ground the gears vigorously, and we leapt forward. In a moment, he was whistling a horse-riding tune, spinning the steering wheel as he swerved around the potholes.

'Next year,' he continued, 'I'll go to Korea. Work two years in a factory, make money. Then I'll come back.'

'What will you do with the money?'

'Buy a car. Hyundai. Very good car. Then I'll be a taxi driver.'

At Tsagaan Sar, the White Month – the lunar New Year and symbolic end of winter – Mongolians launch into vigorous spring cleaning. That spring, all the talk was of cleaning out politics, clearing out corruption. An audit had found that millions of dollars' worth of Mongolia's lifeline of foreign aid had been misappropriated or was simply missing. Parliament – in its most decisive act in more than a year – had changed its mind about gambling and sent the Macau casino mob packing. The newspapers alleged that MPs had been bribed into supporting the casino with money, cars and free trips. A police investigation began that would lead to three Democrat MPs being tried and jailed for corruption.

A new group of Democrat politicians came forward, vowing to scrub the slime from Mongolian politics. I met one of them in the spring. Oyun had been an MP only for a few months, but she was already a political celebrity: young, Cambridge educated, with angular cheekbones and fine features that revealed her mixed Russian and Mongolian blood. Like her brother, Zorig.

Oyun had been working in London when her brother was murdered. She had returned home and run for his seat in parliament, which she easily won. She was now one of a group of MPs calling for a crackdown on corruption: tougher penalties for graft, an independent sleaze-fighting authority.

I met her in a near-empty hotel dining room swimming in cutlery and white napkins. There were two questions I really wanted to ask. The first – so who killed your brother? – I just couldn't. So I asked the second: how bad was corruption in Mongolia?

She gave a measured politician's answer. 'There's no smoke without fire,' she said in her perfect English. 'Definitely there have been corrupt practices, during the previous MPRP government and in this one as well.

The problem is, they have never been brought to justice or brought to light.

'Mongolia is a small country. It's in a transition period. Society hasn't fully stabilised yet. It hasn't really transferred from one system to another yet. In a small country like this, just making a few big decisions which are not based on national interest but on personal interest, it can have such a bad impact on the whole country. You can just bribe a few officials – just three or four people can have a disastrous impact on the whole country. That's why it's so important to do something.

'We have to change people's attitudes so they understand something can be done about corruption. Because currently it seems many people think things are bad and there's nothing they can do about it. People have to understand that something can be done – not that corruption can be eliminated, but it can at least be restricted or controlled.

'If we don't start doing something now, then it's the beginning of the end, and the public should understand that. Maybe it's a lifelong fight, but if you don't start . . .'

Strong, sensible words. But in a poor country, with meagre resources, temptation is hard to resist.

A week later, on a radiant spring morning, I went to the unveiling of Zorig's memorial statue in downtown Ulaanbaatar, in front of the headquarters of his party and opposite the hulking Central Post Office. A large crowd was jostling around the perimeter rope; inside it stood politicians, dignitaries, family. The shroud was whipped off the statue. The design had been controversial since it was deliberately unheroic, depicting Zorig as he had been in life: papers under his arm, Stewardess cigarette in his fingers. The black monument was blessed by a group of monks in their gold and maroon robes; a military band, blinding in scarlet and blue, played the national anthem. A little shakily. Oyun and her surviving brother flanked their mother, each clasping an elbow as the tiny, frail Russian woman wept uncontrollably. I thought the politicians shifted uneasily.

Afterwards, we lined up to file past the statue, deposit our flowers, and mumble something to the family. The family soon went home, but the line-up stayed all week. Every time I passed by, there was a queue around the statue and its growing floral mountain. People would approach, leave a bouquet or packet of Stewardess cigarettes, then grab a private instant with the statue, reaching out a hand to touch the stone for a moment – exactly as Mongolians do to a champion wrestler or a race-winning horse.

One day, a middle-aged man came up beside me as I stood watching.

'It's such a shame,' he said. 'Corruption is everywhere, in plain sight.'

'Is it the Democrats' fault?' I asked.

'It's not just because of democracy,' he said emphatically. 'The democratic leaders aren't the only ones taking bribes. The roots are in the Communist period. For seventy years, corruption was secret; it has just come to light in the democratic period.'

'That's progress,' I suggested.

He shrugged his shoulders and walked off.

Chapter Six

The Four Seasons

Chris, the Australian journalist, and I were having a discussion about weather forecasting. He said nostrils freezing was 20 °C below; eyelashes freezing was 30 °C below. 'Look! My eyelashes are freezing!' He pointed to the evidence.

Chris was from Melbourne. For him, the Mongolian winter had passed rapidly from exciting novelty to dull shock. In an effort to cope, he had taken to wearing the World's Ugliest Coat. It was a handmade Mongolian affair, with corduroy on the outside and on the inside sheepskin so fresh from the sheep that it appeared still to be growing. It hung down from the hem like rogue pubic hair.

Me, I'd tried to make do with my old southern Ontario winter coat. Adapting it for Mongolia required many insulating layers of turtleneck, T-shirt and long underwear. In the end, I looked like a beach ball.

If you know anything about Mongolia, it's likely to be that it's cold. The only thing about the country I remember learning in school is that it has the coldest national capital in the world – in other words, Ulaanbaatar is the only capital city more frigid than Ottawa.

I was not reassured when, shortly after I'd arrived in the country, a young Mongolian woman at a party said to me, 'Oh, Siberia! They have wonderful winters there compared to here.'

It didn't disappoint. The first snow fell on 15 September. Soon after, the last scraps of warmth bled out of the still-plentiful sunshine.

Every morning between October and April, I'd bundle up in my 500 layers and my cashmere scarf and hat – a process that took about a quarter of an hour – and scuttle the half mile to work, skating dangerously across the thick ice that covered roads, paths and pavements. I'd arrive blue with cold, shivering and whining.

Gradually I realised that I was the only one in the office complaining about the weather. This struck me as one of the fundamental differences between Mongolians and Canadians. Mongolians are masters of winter. They make it look so easy. And they do it in style. The colder it gets, the better they look.

I soon became familiar with the key fashion groups on display on Ulaanbaatar's streets. There was the Classic: a traditional *del* lined with sheepskin for winter and accompanied by knee-high leather boots. Perfect for riding your horse or your Russian Planeta motorcycle. Then there was Youth Style: fluorescent down-filled puffa jackets and cashmere toques. My favourite was the style, worn by men and women alike, that I thought of as Soviet Chic: ankle-length leather coats, sunglasses and big furry hats. My office had a shelf above the coat rack that on cold days held a neat row of identical fur hats. It looked like the small-mammal display at the Natural History Museum.

Mongolia is no place for vegetarians or animal-rights activists. With more than 30 million head of livestock, the country is a major producer of fur, cashmere and other animal products. Skins and furs are key to winter comfort and survival. In the State Department Store in Ulaanbaatar – a wonderful old communist holdover with surly staff and byzantine purchasing procedures – you could choose from mounds of disturbingly lifelike fur hats or buy a fur coat (animal of origin uncertain) for £70. At Mongolia's annual fashion awards, the design categories were wool, leather and fur.

Mongolians, I soon realised, are an altogether tougher lot than Canadians. I put it down to centuries of harsh nomadic living compounded by decades of Communist authoritarianism. They simply refused to moan. The difference was brought home to me one Friday afternoon in January, when word went around the office that we were all to come in on Saturday morning to clear the ice from the pavement in front of our building.

'What? On a weekend?' I asked, a bit incredulous. The government had only just abolished the six-day work week, and I was unwilling to surrender my new-found weekend freedom.

Yes, I was told. The city government had decreed that every business, office, and school was responsible for clearing the ice for 50 yards around its premises, by Monday.

'Doesn't the city do it?' I asked. Silly question. Where would it get the money?

If others were upset by the intrusion, they didn't show it. But while I sat sputtering over the loss of my Saturday morning lie-in, my officemates whispered to one another and sent delegations to management, negotiating a compromise. Soon it was announced that we would not have to come in on Saturday. We would be allowed to take part of the afternoon off and break the ice then.

Still slightly disbelieving, I bundled on my coat, gloves, and hat and followed everyone out into the -30°C afternoon. The company bookkeeper-turned-foreman waited by the gate, handing out shovels, metal poles and pieces of cardboard. We spread out in a line along the pavement, some smashing the hard-packed ice with shovels or poles while others swept the shards into piles with the cardboard.

Breaking up a sheet of ice about three inches thick is hard work. Soon my ears and nose were numb, and I'd ripped holes in my cashmere gloves. But I could see that whining just wasn't going to go down. Next to me was a woman, seven months pregnant, wearing a full-length leather coat and chatting and joking as she smashed away.

'What the hell do they think this is?' I muttered to myself. '*Communism?*'

But while the Russian-imposed social system goes some way toward explaining Mongolians' uncomplaining acceptance of unpaid mass labour, their expert handling of the hardships of winter is much older and deeper. (The other thing to be said is that it was much easier to walk to work the next Monday, with the pavement's skating-rink surface hacked away.)

Mongolians have a relationship to the seasons that is . . . *organic*, for want of a better word. They know winter – with its crisp, crystal-clear days and piercing Siberian winds, its late snows and sudden cold snaps that can kill young or weak livestock – intimately.

'Don't worry,' my colleague Oyuna reassured me one day at the office when I looked particularly sniffly and miserable. 'We're almost through the coldest nine days now.'

Mongolia's traditional lunar calendar, she explained, divides winter into nine phases of nine days. Each phase has a name, from 'lambs must be covered' to 'not cold enough to freeze soup.' We were now almost through 'brass monkey balls just about hanging on' (or some such); soon it would warm up.

I took some comfort in this, until Oyuna went on to tell me that the winter cycle ended with the lunar New Year festival of Tsagaan Sar, the White Month. The lunar New Year fell in late January or early February. It seemed insanely optimistic to call that the beginning of spring.

But perhaps it's a half-empty, half-full thing. While central Mongolia does not see new leaves, budding flowers, and other traditional signs of spring until late May or early June, the weather does tend to warm up markedly in late February. From then on, days above the freezing point grow more frequent, and the bone-chilling -20s and -30s have been banished for another year.

In any case, I'm convinced that Mongolians prefer winter to all other seasons. Like all cold-climate peoples, they are in large measure defined by it. I have often thought that Gilles Vigneault's lovely Québécois song – 'Mon pays ce n'est pas un pays, c'est l'hiver' – would make a fine anthem for Mongolia.

The freezing temperatures were no deterrent to outdoor activities. In my neighbourhood, a row of blocks of flats marching up a hill, children sledded terrifyingly down the pavement on cafeteria trays and bits of cardboard box. In Ulaanbaatar's main park, they skated on a drained pond studded with outcrops of rock. All over the city, vendors sold ice-cream bars and ready-made cones out of cardboard boxes. People scarfed them down.

A popular winter weekend trip for office groups (travelling in rust-bucket Czech buses) and Nordic-leaning expats (travelling in shiny four-wheel drives) was Moose (Handgait in Mongolian, but it sounds so much better in English), a park in a wooded valley north of Ulaanbaatar where you could rent heavy, lethal-looking sleds and chipped wooden cross-country skis. Foreigners would struggle into the skis and trudge off up the valley. Mongolians would clamber up the steep tobogganing hill behind the rental shack and whoosh back down – into the car park – to a cacophony of shouts and horns. Then they'd march back up the hill to do it again.

Many people would simply stay in the car park and have a picnic. By late afternoon, some of the men would have stripped to the waist for an impromptu wrestling tournament.

On these crisp afternoons – as long as I never stopped moving – it was possible to see past the cold and appreciate the piercing beauty of the Mongolian winter with its pure blue skies and short but brilliant sunsets.

In Ulaanbaatar, it was a lot harder. Mongolia's capital

is set in a valley and powered by coal. The city's Soviet planners had, perversely, built the belching power stations in the west end of town, so the prevailing winds spread a blanket of smoke over the city. Add thousands of *gers*, each with its own coal stove, and the result was a haze as thick as a London fog (and an alarming rate of respiratory infection) – in a country with almost no heavy industry and one of the world's lowest population densities.

But in Mongolia, I found, even pollution can be beautiful. Ulaanbaatar is a low-rise city, so even in the centre of town you can see a vast expanse of sky. During winter sunsets, the sun burnished the smog into a delicate shade of pink, like a candy floss blanket over the city.

The approach of spring unleashes all sorts of dangers. During my first winter in Mongolia, the lamas charged with setting the date for the lunar New Year celebrations announced that Tsagaan Sar would be held during the last week of February – a full month later than the Chinese lunar New Year. (Although the stars were invoked, I suspected the real reason was a reflexive desire to differ from the Chinese.) The postponement led to the Thawing Dumpling Scare, which filled many columns of newsprint in the run-up to the holiday.

Tsagaan Sar is one of the two biggest holidays in the Mongolian calendar (the other is the summer sports-based festival, Naadam), and in many ways it is the most beloved, revolving as it does around three things central to Mongolian life: family, food and drink. Everyone spends the three days of the holiday (and often several days more) dropping in on friends, neighbours and family. In each home, a lavish spread will be laid out: piles of biscuits, bowls of sweets and sugar cubes, a rump of mutton, bottles of vodka.

But the centrepiece of Tsagaan Sar gluttony is *buuz*, a kind of steamed mutton dumpling the size of a child's fist that is the country's national dish. Mongolians have a bottomless appetite for *buuz*, and it's no exaggeration to say that a typical family will prepare hundreds of them in the days before New Year. A friend told me that she and her sister made more than a thousand, spending many evenings going through the same motions: place a dollop of minced mutton, perhaps mixed with chopped onion or garlic, on a circle of dough. Fold over, pinch closed (experienced *buuz* cooks pride themselves on their distinctive signature pinching patterns).

Mongolians do not have large freezers – most do not have freezers at all – but, happily, Mongolian winter means that the dumplings may simply be stored, frozen, outside until the big day. In the weeks before Tsagaan Sar, the balconies of Ulaanbaatar sag under bags of *buuz*.

But as February ran out, the temperature began creeping up toward the freezing point. It set off a national crisis. Newspapers reported that untold thousands of *buuz* were in danger of spoilage. The Institute of Meteorology and Hydrology released frequent, detailed weather bulletins. The nation held its breath.

In the end, it was all right. Spring held off until after

the holiday, and there were no cases of *buuz* poisoning. No reported cases, at any rate.

Around the world, spirits soar at the approach of spring, with its promise of new life and regeneration. But it is Mongolia's least favourite time of year, a mad season of turmoil and worry.

I noticed this lack of enthusiasm around the end of March. I asked Oyuna, who was raised in the countryside and was a trove of meteorological lore, what accounted for the feeling of unease.

'We don't like spring,' she confirmed. 'It's a very . . .' She searched for the right word. 'A very hot time.' She didn't mean the temperature. 'We Mongolians are very affected by the seasons. In winter, nothing happens. Everybody just wants to stay at home.'

With the spring thaw, it all comes gushing out. I began to understand this a few weeks later when, all of a sudden, the government resigned. I was mystified. The Democratic Coalition, elected less than two years earlier, had a two-thirds majority in parliament. Sure, there had been sporadic anti-government demonstrations since autumn, but most of them had mustered no more than a few dozen hard-hit pensioners. Most people I spoke to seemed fond of chubby, affable Prime Minister Enkhsaikhan. Why had he and his cabinet just stepped down en masse?

Oyuna just shrugged. 'Spring,' she said. The natural season of agitation and instability. The demonstrations that had cracked open the old Communist regime in 1990 – those had taken place in springtime. So if Enkhsaikhan's rivals within the coalition were to push out the PM, install their own man in the top job, and appoint a new cabinet of pliable backbenchers, it could happen in no other season.

Spring in Mongolia is not all green shoots and warming soil. It is dangerous, even treacherous. Winter is nothing if not consistent: crisp, cold and sunny. Spring is troublingly unpredictable. It can bring gales, hail, rain, snow and dust storms – sometimes all in the same day.

In contrast to the season's symbolism in most countries, spring in Mongolia is the season of death, a time for herders to watch the sky and worry. The uneasy transition from winter to spring is the most dangerous time of all. A bout of severe weather can wipe out a generation of lambs, kids, foals and calves (and, indeed, wildlife. In 1999, it was reported that 90 per cent of the antelopes born that spring had died, largely as a result of hoof rot induced by heavy rains).

The Mongolian language has a word for one common and dreaded winter-spring phenomenon: *zuud*. That one syllable is defined as a cold snap and snowfall following a period of thaw. The sudden chill freezes melting snow into a hard crust of ice, which young and winter-weakened livestock cannot break to reach the grass. Many thousands of animals can die during a *zuud*.

It's a phenomenon that underscores how precarious the lives of most Mongolians remain, even in the twenty-first century. As if to illustrate the point, the dawn of the new millennium brought Mongolia the most cataclysmic *zuud* in living memory. It was the result of an unfortunate confluence of meteorological factors. An unusually dry spring and hot summer, which had withered the pasture land across a large swath of the country, had been followed by an exceptionally cold winter with heavy snowfalls. The result was that livestock – which must eat constantly in autumn to fatten up for the long winter ahead – were weak, and the snow was deep. By March, nearly 2 million of the country's 30 million head of livestock were dead.

This was – it's no exaggeration – a national disaster. Many herders in the worst-hit areas lost almost all their animals: sheep, goats, cows and horses. Come summer, they would have no dairy products, no meat to preserve for winter, no dung to burn for fuel, no means of transportation. Nothing.

Unlike an earthquake or a forest fire, this disaster took a long time to happen. The herders saw it coming. But so weak is Mongolia's communications infrastructure, so feeble and disorganised is the government's ability to respond – and, it's tempting to add, so unobservant are many of the myriad aid agencies – that almost nothing was done until it was too late, until thousands of herders stood staring at the piles of carcasses outside their *gers*, contemplating the ruin of their livelihoods.

The more experienced, far-sighted herders had taken steps to prepare themselves. In the autumn, they slaughtered large numbers of animals in order to stockpile meat, or moved far from their traditional homes in search of secure pasture. In the worst-hit province, Middle Gobi, almost half the population left. Those who remained were often the young and the old or the least experienced – city-raised Mongolians who had little knowledge of cattle rearing but had returned to the land in the belief that as long as they had animals they would not starve. Now they faced starvation.

Even if the rains were generous, new grass would not grow until May or June, and by then there would be few animals left for the herders to slaughter in preparation for the coming winter. It would take years to recover.

One government official in the Middle Gobi summed it up to a United Nations delegation: 'Whatever economic gains we've made since the end of the Communist era a decade ago will be wiped out.'

Less cataclysmic but also dangerous are the winds that rake the steppe each spring and whip up blinding, stinging dust storms. Much of Mongolia is desert or semidesert; during a dust storm, it can feel positively Saharan.

Dust storms often strike without warning. One spring weekend, a group of us decided the weather was perfect for a picnic. Saturday was warm, sunny and glorious, T-shirt weather at last. We decided that on Sunday we'd pack a lunch and drive two hours out of town to a reserve for Przywalski horses. These wild animals had long been extinct in their Mongolian habitat but were being reintroduced from zoos in Europe. I'd seen photos of the stubby, fawn-coloured creatures and found them oddly compelling. Their necks were a little too thick, their heads a little too big – they looked like a child's drawing or an imperfect prototype for a horse. I was keen to see them in the flesh.

Sunday morning was slightly overcast but still warm.

We set off in our Russian jeep along the pitted road out of town. A few miles west of Ulaanbaatar, the wind began to blow. Then it began to howl, and suddenly the landscape turned sepia.

The driver turned on the headlights, but still we could see no more than a yard ahead, at what looked like a solid wall of sand. The drone drowned out the jeep's engine, no mean feat. We inched forward. Several times we had to pull over until a gap appeared in the sand. Once, the driver got out to pee, an accomplishment we appreciated when we tried to get out ourselves. We could scarcely stand up.

By the time we reached the reserve, the wind had dropped enough for us to make out the shapes of several *gers* set in a river valley surrounded by rocky hills. Several of the *gers* had large new rips in their white canvas covers.

The park director was clearly surprised to have visitors on a day that was plainly not good for anything but sitting around the stove drinking tea, but he had encountered the eccentricities of foreigners before. He let us sit in his office to eat our sandwiches and chew over the ruins of our picnic. He even joined us in the jeep and directed us half a mile down a track to where a clump of wild horses – the correct term is harem, he informed us – stood close together on a hillside. They were hard to spot at first, being the colour of sand themselves. They were grazing calmly, stoically snatching at clumps of grass that tore past their mouths. But then these were the ancestors of domestic Mongolian horses, the indestructible creatures that conquered the world in the time of Chinggis Khan.

With that thought, we headed home to soak the grit out of our pores.

After all this, Mongolians greet summer with relief and maybe a touch of discomfort.

It was all very sudden. Spring went on, week after windswept week. Then, seemingly overnight, the larches burst forth in loud green, the grass grew rich and thick, the sun beat down, and I started to sweat. It was the end of June. It was summer. It was over 30 °C.

At last, my Mongolian colleagues began to complain. They arrived at work flushed and damp and saying, 'Hot enough for you?' In the countryside, the animals swatted flies listlessly in the fields. In the city, people sweated listlessly on patios. It was great.

The only thing that prevented the whole country from sinking into a stupor was Naadam. The national Naadam in Ulaanbaatar lasts for three days and centres on competitions in Mongolia's 'three manly sports': wrestling, horse racing and archery.

It's a gruelling business, especially the horse racing, as I was reminded at a small regional Naadam as I stood by the finish line waiting for the tide of horse flesh to come sweeping in. One of the leading horses crossed the line and collapsed, twitching. A crowd of men gathered around while the tiny jockey was led away, wailing.

Naadam is not for the faint of heart. Postholiday reports in the Ulaanbaatar press contained accounts of how many horses had died during the races and of how many spectators had drowned in the Tuul River while attempting to cool off.

Having been warned of the unbearable heat and the hordes of (God forbid!) tourists at the Naadam stadium in Ulaanbaatar, I elected to spend the holiday in the countryside, camping and taking in local games. There was no stadium, just a circle of tents providing shade around the wrestling field, and the competitors were so close that spectators had to leap out of the way every time one made a lunge.

Retreating to the perimeter of spectators, I came across a tall and craggy European unloading polo equipment from the back of a Land Cruiser, as if this were the most normal thing in the world to be doing in the middle of the Asian steppe.

'What on earth are you doing?' I asked.

Reintroducing polo to Mongolia. Of course.

'We think the Mongols used to play polo in Genghis Khan's time, you see, but the tradition has been lost. So we've got together some players from Britain and India, and we're going to have a bit of a demonstration. We've a few Mongolians in the group as well; they took to it very quickly.'

I had to admit that it was a natural sport for a nation practically born on horseback. And the demonstration match gathered quite a crowd, who watched with enthusiasm before heading back to the wrestling.

I returned to work after the holiday to find Oyuna looking perkier than she had in weeks.

'Good holiday?' I asked.

'Oh, yes,' she said. 'You know, we Mongolians say autumn begins after Naadam.'

'But it's the middle of July!'

'Yes,' she said cheerfully. 'Soon it will grow cool again.'

And things, she seemed to suggest, can then get back to normal.

Chapter Seven

Young, Wild and Free

'Jilly,' said Bilguun, all seriousness. 'What is the meaning of the expression 'Welcome to my world'?'

Baby Bilguun, 18 years old and five foot two, the cut of his hair as sharp as the crease in his trousers, his leather shoes blinding, was the *UB Post*'s layout artist and cub reporter. Or would have been, except that he spent more time buffing his shoes to a brilliant shine than he did reporting. In a nation obsessed with keeping its footwear clean, he had the most dazzling loafers I ever saw.

He knocked the layout off in one afternoon a week. The rest of the time he rustled about the office, disappearing for long stretches – planning. He had ambitions to go to America, and with his youthful verve and nearly convincing air of cunning I knew he wouldn't be with us for long.

It was too bad; he was great company. He had the best English of anyone on staff, picked up from an American teacher at his high school and careful study of the lyrics of the Backstreet Boys. (I had some difficulty persuading him that 'Welcome to my world' was not a phrase to be used as an everyday greeting. In fact, I don't think I did convince him, and so winning was his insouciant air that it may well have gone down a treat when he did get to the States.)

Bilguun was every bit my idea of the New Mongolian: confident, Westward-looking, remorselessly self-improving. Mongolia is a nation of autodidacts – I sometimes wondered whether this was an act of rebellion, nurtured out of sight of a succession of occupiers, or simply the product of an isolated, rather lonely existence. I often met people with passions for genealogy or history or foreign languages. Especially foreign languages. As I struggled to find any sense in the rustling shwoosh of spoken Mongolian, I wondered at their sponge-like ability to absorb languages: first Russian, now English. Bilguun was typical. I could almost see his vocabulary growing, day by day.

Like thousands of other young Mongolians, Bilguun was determined to go to the United States and grab fistfuls of experience, excitement and cash. It was a dream he pursued with a mixture of ruthlessness and innocence. He was undaunted by his youth, his lack of education, his absence of firsthand experience of a capitalist country, or the draconian stance of the US Embassy's visa section.

'I must be a very foxy guy, like my father,' the dapper, diminutive teenager told me over warm Mongolian beer one evening before his departure. His father was a well-known nationalist poet and activist for Mongolian language and literature who had been sent into internal exile in the Gobi desert during one of the Communist era's periodic purges. He had endured and was once again a man of influence. 'Of course, I will do some crimes,' Bilguun added with a guileless smile. Leaning across the table, he told me one of his plans.

The Americans had sent Mongolia a shipment of cattle medicine as aid, he said. In the United States, the stuff went for US$1,200 a litre. In Mongolia, it was being sold for $200. Bilguun's father, conveniently, was a half brother of the minister of agriculture. He had 'purchased' 100 litres of the shipment on a promise to pay $20,000. Bilguun had shipped it to the United States – in someone else's name, of course. For taking the risk, the third party would get $8,000. Bilguun would then go to America, collect the stuff, and sell it to American farmers for $800 a litre. After paying off his father and the mule, he would have $52,000 dollars. He thought he might use the money to attend Harvard or Georgetown.

I had no idea how much of this was true. I tried to imagine this Mongolian kid approaching Midwestern farmers with his cut-price cattle medicine and a tale about how it had fallen off the back of a tractor. I wasn't sure whether he was a smooth operator or a babe in the woods. I knew he must have had some clout just to get a visa and several thousand dollars to pay the tuition for the English course he was supposedly going to take. The US Embassy had cracked down on Mongolian English students in response to a near-universal overstay rate. Bilguun did not seem to be concerned.

The next week, a three-month student visa in his hand and his pet turtle in his pocket, he flew to San Francisco.

'What will you miss most about Mongolia?' I asked him.

'Taking taxis everywhere,' he replied without hesitation.

Two years later, he was still in the States.

In Ulaanbaatar, I was constantly meeting kids like Bilguun: confident, intrepid, naive. Mongolia is a nation teeming with youth. The Communist regime's drives to increase the birth rate – including the awarding of Glorious Mother medals to women who had five or more children – were startlingly effective; by the 1980s, the country had a growth rate of 2.5 per cent. (Needless to say, such policies are now in disrepute, and the growth rate has fallen to about 1.5 per cent. But their passing is frequently lamented by media commentators, who reflect the commonly held view that what Mongolia needs is about 8 million more Mongolians.)

Today, half the country's population is under 21; 40 per cent is under 16. In the capital, the young were everywhere: roller-blading across Sukhbaatar Square, queuing up to get into nightclubs such as Top 10 and the Hard Rock, hauling huge jugs of water to their family's *ger*, herding livestock on the scraggly grass by the river.

These kids were a new breed of hybrid Mongolian, the products of nomadic tradition, Soviet Communism, and an exhilarating cocktail of new influences, influences whose traces were writ large on the walls of Ulaanbaatar's Soviet apartment blocks: graffiti ensuring there is one corner of Mongolia that is forever KURT COBAIN, BOB MARLEY (actually BOB MARLEE), and CRADLE OF FILTH and hand-painted signs advertising SEGA for rent in a ground-floor flat. New wavelengths were beamed into the homes of the nascent middle class on video and DVD, on cable and satellite television: MTV, CNN, BBC, Russian game shows,

Latin American soaps and Hollywood musicals. *Oprah*. Even dull, threadbare Mongol Television had taken to broadcasting bootleg copies of the latest Hollywood releases, enthusiastically dubbed by Mongolian actors. Young Mongolians were wasting no time catching up on what they'd missed, giving themselves an ad hoc education in Western pop culture. I met one young man who was engaged in translating *Easy Rider* for broadcast on Mongolian TV. 'What exactly,' he asked me, 'is the difference between 'cool' and 'groovy'?'

(The picture quality on these films was always appalling. I watched a version of *Titanic* that had clearly been filmed covertly in a cinema; along the bottom of the screen you could make out the heads of the people in the front row.)

I was more surprised, though, by the country's vibrant home-grown pop scene: posses of shiny young boy bands and girl groups cutting CDs and dancing in sync in discos and Palaces of Culture. I was a bit distressed by their wholesale imitation of Western commercial pop – one dose of girl group Spike was all it took to convince me the last thing the world needed was a Mongolian-language Spice Girls – but I was heartened by their energy and enthusiasm. No Western band was ever going to tour Mongolia; they would have to do it themselves.

In fact, one Western band did play Mongolia: Smokie. You may well have forgotten this minor 1970s outfit from the north of England (I had), but you might retain a trace memory of their parasitically catchy big hits, 'Stumblin' In' and 'Living Next Door to Alice' (I did.

Don't worry, I won't sing them for you). In the West, Smokie is a trivia question. In Mongolia, they are rock gods.

In the 1970s and 1980s, Mongolian radio did not play Western pop music – there was a handful of government-approved home-grown groups – but many young Mongolians went to study in the relatively sophisticated countries of Eastern Europe, and Smokie was big in Germany. The cassettes they brought back were passed excitedly from hand to teenage hand.

'In the seventies and eighties,' one sophisticated woman in her twenties told me, 'we knew two Western bands: The Beatles and Smokie.'

Smokie is *the* nostalgia band for Mongolia's Generation X. One summer, the aging icons were flown in to play a show at the national stadium in Ulaanbaatar – a minor band, maybe, but a major coup for the new breed of Mongolian promoter-entrepreneur. The event received breathless blanket coverage in the press, and from the moment the band – five middle-aged men with the bodies of bricklayers and the hair of Roger Daltrey – stepped off the plane, they were besieged by children, students, businesspeople and the speaker of parliament.

The band was booked to play the biggest venue in town, the 15,000-seat open-air national stadium. The day of the show dawned rainy, but the clouds lifted in late afternoon, and by evening the park around the stadium had taken on the air of a carnival: thousands of families milled about; vendors sold fried mutton dumplings and fizzy drinks; hundreds of police officers in berets and navy bomber jackets ringed the building, looking self-important and fingering their truncheons. Smokie was accorded a level of security suitable to a visiting head of state. Inside the stadium, as the stands filled up and a handful of Mongolian bands warmed up the crowd with their own renditions of Smokie classics (that's a novel idea, I thought; let the opening acts steal all your best songs), groups of students settled down on the grass and unpacked picnics: dumplings, potato salad, biscuits, thermoses of tea.

The whole thing was as naive and good natured and uncynical as could be. And maybe I'd been in Mongolia too long, but as I stood amid the jostling, glo-stick-waving crowd listening to Smokie's low-cal guitar rock, I kind of thought they rocked.

When it was over and the band had left the stage, everyone applauded, then stood still and waited. At length Smokie's tour van appeared, flanked by an escort of police vehicles and a squad of soldiers who jogged alongside the van. As the band made its way across the stadium toward the gate, the crowd surged forward – then stopped at a respectful distance, leaving a corridor through which the vehicle and its bemused-looking occupants could pass, and waved.

For many young Mongolians in the countryside, and a fair few in the cities, the arrival of the brave new MTV world has brought bizarre juxtapositions. A friend of mine went to live in the westernmost village in Mongolia. It was a tiny community, remote even by Mongolia's extreme standards, more than 900 miles from Ulaanbaatar: several days' drive over unpaved tracks. The people there received little in the way of services from, and had little contact with, the government in Ulaanbaatar. She met people who couldn't name the prime minister of Mongolia. But they rushed around in distress one day to tell her that Ginger Spice had left the Spice Girls.

I'm not sure how far this knowledge goes toward mitigating the increasingly difficult lives of many young Mongolians. One family I visited on the northern edge of the Gobi desert had two children, a girl and a boy. The girl of about eight was chatty and exuberant, drawing pictures on which she wrote titles before signing her name with a flourish. But her older brother could not write his name. His sister went to school in the provincial capital, but he had been kept at home to help tend the herds. He watched his sister draw for a few moments, then picked up a bow and arrow, leapt on his horse, and galloped off to hunt marmots. The boy's father could read – I saw him poring over a two-week-old newspaper – but his son could not.

Mongolia is justifiably proud of its literacy rate of over 90 per cent; it is one of the genuine achievements of the Communist period. Under Communism, rural children were sent to board at schools in provincial towns. Today school supplies cost money, one thing most herding families lack.

So, many children must go to work. Mongolia does not have high-profile, media-grabbing child labourers in industrial sweatshops – it scarcely has any factories. It does have thousands of rural children working as herders and thousands of urban kids shining shoes, selling newspapers, or hauling goods in crowded marketplaces.

One blustery late-winter day, I went to Nalaikh, a crumbling coal town 20 miles east of Ulaanbaatar, with David, an American photographer in search of images of child labourers.

Defunct mining towns, whether in northern Ontario or in central Mongolia, all have the same poignant air of abandonment and faded glory. Nalaikh was typical slapdash urban Mongolia, all dirt roads and chipped concrete. The abandoned mine buildings, with their huge brick chimneys and crumbling walls, sat on a hill, looming over the community with the eerie grandeur of a ruined castle.

We walked up to the old mine, which had had its own railway spur line and neat little station. For years, this mine had supplied the capital with its coal. Many of the workers were ethnic Kazakhs from the far west of Mongolia who had been lured east by the promise of jobs. When Communism fell and the economy collapsed, the mine was privatised, then closed.

Nearly all the adult men in town had worked in the mine. We had heard that many still did, going underground with picks and shovels to scrape out the coal that remained.

Up close, the mine looked spookily, almost stereotypically, abandoned. Above us spread a forest of creaking branches of cable and girder; underfoot, black scree and twisted metal. But almost immediately we ran into a pair of young men, leaning against the remains of a wall, who were happy to tell us about their work. They confirmed that the mine site was still worked by gangs of local men who had informally divided it up. This was their shaft. They dug the coal seam, about 15 yards below the surface, using explosives, picks, and shovels during the winter, until the thaw, when the ground grew soft and the work became too dangerous. They kept some of the coal to heat their own homes but sold most of it to traders from the city. The price wasn't very good, but it was better than nothing.

A few yards away, stooped men emerged from a hole with bags slung over their shoulders. They emptied them into the back of an old Russian truck.

'How old are the miners?' we asked.

'All ages,' said one young man.

'Even young kids?'

'Not here,' he said sharply, 'but some of the other crews have kids as young as eight on them. Over there' – he pointed to a hole a few hundred yards away – 'there's a 13-year-old boy working.'

We thanked them.

'Mind you don't fall into a hole!' one shouted after us.

We approached the other shaft just in time to see a small boy emerge, doubled up under a sack that looked bigger than he was. David crouched down to get what would have been a terrific shot had he not been interrupted by the foreman: snarling, charging, and brandishing a shovel, which he used to thump Ariunbat, our translator, on the chest. We retreated.

Some minutes later, and rather more cautiously, we strolled up to a third work crew a few hundred yards away, this one manned by Mongolian Kazakhs.

Two young men in leather jackets and sunglasses were standing beside a truck. Their shoes were polished, their jeans new. They were the city traders. They paid the miners 20,000 tugrug for a truckload of coal, which they sold in Ulaanbaatar for 50,000 tugrug. It was then packaged and sold to capital residents for 1,500 tugrug a bag. Pretty good money for doing, effectively, nothing.

The traders watched as miners dressed in coal-caked sweatshirts and toques placed the last sacks in the back of the truck. Before they drove off, one tilted his chin in the direction of the miners. 'Watch out – they're Kazakhs,' he said with a laugh.

On Ariunbat's instructions, we stood around, looking casual, saying nothing. This went on for some time, but I had been in Mongolia long enough not to get frustrated. The situation was evolving. After a few moments, Ariunbat exchanged pleasantries with the miners. A few minutes later, cigarettes were passed around. After half an hour, the miners were chatting and joking and queuing to pose for David atop their ever-growing mound of coal.

The men took turns heading down the 100-yard tunnel to haul the sacks of coal to the surface. Each miner made about 120 trips a day.

'People started digging up the coal in '93, when the mine closed,' the foreman, a muscular man in his fifties, said. 'The closure threw two thousand people out of work. That means their whole families. I worked in the mine for eleven years. It was a good wage. Now we don't make a great salary. It's just to survive. I'd say there are several thousand people working over the whole site. We work every day, even on weekends.

'Sure, it's dangerous – three or four people die here ever year – but what can we do? If we don't work, we'll starve.'

He said his crew ranged in age from 13 to 56. I approached the youngest miner, 13-year-old Batsaikhan, an Artful Dodger lookalike in baggy clothes and a thick coat of coal dust. He said he'd been working as a miner for two years. He was the oldest of five children in his family; his father was unemployed. He had never been to school.

'How do you feel about your work?' I asked.

He was quiet for a long moment. 'I like it. It's . . . tough. I feel like an adult.'

Both his younger brothers were eager to follow him underground.

'And what do you want to be when you grow up?'

That didn't require much thought. 'A miner,' he said.

The miners led us down the tunnel into a series of coal chambers. Perhaps a dozen men were working the coal face; they had three helmets and lamps between them. By now we were all pals. They let us wear the helmets and swing the picks; they posed for pictures, beaming.

One wiry boy shook my hand warmly. He said his name was Balaban, that he was 19 – though he looked much younger – and had worked in the mine for four years. He was fiercely proud of it, I could tell; his pride glowed in the dark.

'It's very interesting work,' he told me intensely. 'Working the rock, digging caves and tunnels.' He grinned. His teeth glinted in the darkness.

Mongolia's youth gives it optimism and exuberance; its history and its geography have given it restraint and endurance. It will swallow big chunks of 'global culture' and add them to the Russian bits and the Chinese bits and all the other bits. But it will always be a place a little apart. At least that is my hope. Mongolia is a country comfortable with being alone with itself, and there is a kind of strength in that.

One night we found ourselves in the village hall in the tiny community of Hatgal: Dave and I and Chris from Australia and Orna from Ireland. It was a drafty wooden barn of a room. It was disco night. The generator had been filled with diesel to drive the music from the erratic tape deck through the crackly speakers. Wooden chairs had been unstacked around the perimeter of the hall. The villagers sat on them, the boys and men with trousers tucked into their stout knee-length leather boots, the girls and women in their best traditional *dels* or in cheap, bright Chinese togs. Occasionally a few of the girls exchanged whispers. The rest were silent.

The DJ, a tall young man with a confident air, knew his audience well. His repertoire alternated between warbly instrumentals, reminiscent of the sounds made by pressing the effects buttons on those electric organs that used to be displayed in department store showrooms – at these the older men and women would waltz gracefully around the hall – and Russian pop songs, during which the youth would rush to the centre of the room and dance in a circle.

We were way out of our league. Chris, a born extrovert, paled under his Australian tan. Orna quickly took a chair and immersed herself in conversation with her Mongolian colleague, Tigi. As I hesitated at the edge of the room and the hall filled with a wavering organ drone, a stocky herder came up and extended his hand. 'Sorry, I don't know how to box-step' was not in my Mongolian vocabulary; I got trod on by his boots and retired humiliated.

Chris was sent flying back into our corner after an athletic spin around the dance floor by a four-foot-eleven *del*-clad dynamo.

'What are we going to do?' he gasped. 'We're the guests of honour. They've turned on the generator just because we came. We can't leave.'

We decided to take pre-emptive action. Chris, a former DJ himself, leapt up on stage and tried to befriend the man behind the tape deck.

'Oasis?' he asked hopefully.

The music man looked blank.

'Backstreet Boys?'

The DJ shook his head sorrowfully.

'Spice Girls?'

'Yesss!' said the DJ.

Chris jumped down beaming. 'He's gonna play 'Wannabe'!'

We quietly celebrated our cultural victory as the DJ rummaged through his plastic cassette cases.

Two Russian divas and one two-step later, the DJ flashed us a thumbs-up. The hall filled with the oddly undulating but unmistakable sound of genuine Western pop music. Chris bolted to the centre of the floor with the air of a man released. Dave and I followed. Only Orna, quicker on the uptake than we were, held back.

We were out on the floor when we realised our terrible mistake. That bassline didn't belong to the perky British pop tarts but to . . . Vanilla Ice. 'Ice, Ice Baby,' intoned history's least convincing white rapper. I glanced around, resigned to dancing in a circle with the youth of Hatgal. But they, every single one, sat around the hall, staring at us with steady, expressionless faces.

We three looked at one another in horror. Then we did the only thing we could do. We danced. For four excruciating minutes, I flailed and posed desperately, while Chris executed the B-boy moves of the damned.

When it was all over, we slunk back to our corner, spent. Our audience neither applauded nor jeered but followed our retreat with even gazes. Except for Orna, who was falling off her chair in hysterics.

Chapter Eight

The Adventurers

They came by the dozens. Tourists. No: travellers. The kind with serious boots. Japanese, North Americans, Europeans. Germans, especially, and Scandinavians.

Not enough of a crowd for anyone but the most rootless, sincere, or desperate to want to stay forever. Enough to make you linger – windswept, waterlogged, broken down, hungry; eating gritty mutton and pot noodles in the countryside; retreating to the city to recuperate and gripe together over your cappuccino in Millie's café – until the weather turned cold, and the Trans-Mongolian Express held the promise of more civilised places. Beijing. Moscow. Places with McDonald's.

Until then, there was Adventure.

A certain kind of city dweller dreams of Mongolia. Land of the harshest climate. The worst roads. Endless grasslands. Snow-capped peaks. Scorching desert. Hardy, hard-bitten nomads. Half-wild horses. Yaks. The toughest country on earth. Land of the brave, home of the free.

You'd stumble across them in summertime. Fuelling up on beer and camaraderie in the city before the arduous journey ahead: eager, confident, primed. Or, later, sitting defeated beside some scorched and dusty track contemplating their runaway horse, blind-drunk driver, or broken-down jeep/motorcycle/mountain bike/ pair of rollerblades.

Their stories always began the same way. 'I've dreamed of Mongolia,' they'd say, 'since . . .' If they were German or Scandinavian, 'since' usually involved some boy's-own story of adventure on the steppe they'd read as a child. For others, it was the image of John Wayne as Chinggis Khan or the ruddy-cheeked nomads in Nikita Mikhailkov's film *Close to Eden*. Mongolia was the last word in rugged. They wanted to test themselves against the greatest Outward Bound course on earth.

In Millie's one day, I met a trim and boyish Japanese man in his early twenties tucking into his lasagne in the company of some friends of mine.

'You'll never guess what he's doing,' they said. 'Tell her, Yoshimi.'

'I am cycling from Japan to Dublin.'

He'd cheated a bit, taken a boat from Osaka to Tianjin, then pedalled inland and north. He'd just crossed the roadless, landmark-free Gobi desert on a mountain bike, pointed northward by helpful herding families who fed the mad waif tea and mutton fat to keep out the night-time cold.

Ahead lay steep hills and broad valleys, 300 miles to the Russian border; and then Siberia, mad Ladas and gangsters; and then Europe, autobahns and speed demons . . .

'Why on earth are you doing it?' I asked.

'When I get there, I will be a man.'

Oh. It was often something like that.

'Our customers,' a veteran tour guide in Ulaanbaatar told me once, 'they've been everywhere. They've done

India, they've done Tibet. Mongolia is their final frontier.'

If Mongolians could bottle the soul-stirring properties of their country for export to understimulated Westerners, they'd grow rich.

'This is my dream,' said Graham, a rangy blond Australian with a grin as big as the Outback and just as intimidating. 'I live for my dreams.'

His particular dream had taken him 1,200 miles on horseback from Ulaanbaatar to the shores of Lake Hovsgol and back during one Mongolian summer and autumn. He was a typical case, an inveterate traveller in his early thirties who had already cycled through China and paddled a canoe among South Pacific islands. As he'd scanned an atlas, Mongolia, a hole at the heart of Asia, had caught his imagination.

'I didn't really know anything about Mongolia to tell you the truth, apart from the empire 700 years ago,' he admitted. 'So why horse-riding across Mongolia? It's the personal challenge. I was scared of horses. There's something about pulling yourself up by your bootstraps, convincing yourself that you can do it.

'I'd worked for five years. It was time for a break. So I quit my job and decided to live out my dream.'

I'd heard that line many times before, and the cynical slacker in me regarded it with deep suspicion. But Graham's dream, at least, was an atypically well-organised one. Unsure of the availability of food in the Mongolian countryside, he'd brought 60 kilograms of supplies from Australia. He'd packed a stack of photos of the Dalai Lama as gifts for the families he visited.

He'd bought maps and a compass and a GPS system, and he'd obtained two horses – one to ride and one to carry his gear. He was also refreshingly modest about his achievement.

'The first month was difficult,' he confessed with a disarming smile. 'I cried. Before I came to Mongolia, I'd only had seven riding lessons. Managing two horses takes some getting used to. Things go wrong: the horses get tangled up, bags fall off, and the horses get scared. It's such a mess. And if things really get messy, the horses get scared and run away. Once I lost both horses in the forest. That was a challenge.'

For the relentlessly optimistic Graham, all setbacks were just challenges he hadn't met yet.

'After the first month, my horsemanship improved to the point where I could manage,' he went on. 'I learned: keep your horses hungry and they won't stray too far. I didn't really have a good night's sleep in five months. I was always sleeping with one ear open. Sometimes I'd wake up and one of the horses had gone walkabout. But I never lost two horses in a night.'

As he spun his tale, I found that I liked Graham. Radiating good health and positive thinking, he was the best advertisement possible for a 1,200-mile horse trek. He almost made me want to try it myself. And he seemed to have come away from his experience refreshingly free of mystical romantic notions about Mongolian herders and with a healthy, unsentimental respect for his hosts and their culture.

'The hospitality was tremendous. People wouldn't let me pass their *ger* without coming in. Sometimes I

only travelled three miles in a day. It's like having a safety
blanket around you, because the herders are so
competent. I can see where the tradition of hospitality
comes from. Life in the countryside is tough. Summer
is just a brief respite from winter.

'My main aim was always to be with the people, but
some nights I would camp on my own, away from a *ger*.
Sometimes you feel like a bit of a break from the fairly
consistent pressure you're under when you're in a *ger*.
You're the entertainment; that's your contribution to
the occasion. I had a picture book of Australia, a horse
magazine, pictures of my family. It took about an hour
and a half to go through that. Very rarely did anybody
speak English, so my Mongolian got very good, within
the limits of what I needed to say: horsey things,
describing Australia.'

Graham's personal philosophy was simple but
fervently held. 'Everything that goes wrong is a
challenge. It's about taking control of your life, breaking
out of a rut and breaking free. I didn't have a goal to go
from east to west or anything. It was just to experience
Mongolia on horseback. There's something special
about travelling through a country by a means of
transport that's so much a part of the culture. By the
end, I was competent with the horses. So, on a personal
level, I felt a sense of achievement. I felt I'd made a
positive impact on the people I'd met, and they'd made
a positive impact on me, and I'd really experienced
Mongolia.'

Graham had had the best possible travel experience,
I thought. He'd come, liked the country – and stayed.

He eventually went back to Australia but returned to Mongolia to start up a travel company, leading hiking, horse-riding and even mountain-biking trips to the countryside. He's still there.

Most other travellers buzzed through on Trans-Siberian stopovers or treated the country like a vast obstacle course, to be motorcycled across or galloped over before they returned to their own countries and their real lives, their normal routines of study or work.

Or they got stuck. It happened a lot. In addition to the migrating flocks of consultants and missionaries (same thing, really) and the briefcase-toting advisors teaching the Mongolians how to run a capitalist economy or make German sausage, Mongolia was full of people who seemed to have been going somewhere and just wandered off the path. The perennial grad student with his thesis on reindeer herders. The French writer with a hinted-at tragic past. The stray Buddhists, shamanists and anthropologists. The odd draft dodger.

You'd see them on the street and say hello, one exile to another, and their eyes would flicker up to yours, wide with surprise, as if you'd startled them out of a reverie. They were people who'd struck their own private relationship with Mongolia, made a personal world to which outsiders were not admitted.

For still others, Mongolia was their own private Siberia.

Across the street from my flat in Ulaanbaatar was the Chinggis Khan Hotel, a pink and black, glass-and-granite monstrosity that sat gleaming and, for most of the year, empty. And inside the hotel was a casino. I'd never lived across the street from a casino before. So I went. You would too. It wasn't Vegas. No slot machines even. Just one large, fern-enhanced room, with German beer and a German chef of legendary girth and temper, a cynical, convivial Yugoslavian manager, and pale, bored Romanian croupiers.

And Jacko. Jacko was Scottish, a talker, and a man who *desperately* wanted to be somewhere else. My friends and I went to the casino once, out of boredom, and Jacko was the reason we went back. He wanted someone to talk to and was willing to buy it with free beer.

Jacko told us some, but far from all, of his background: casinos in Moscow and Sarajevo; a bar in Moscow, too, famed among expats; and a failed joint ownership of a bar in Vietnam, followed by a hasty exit from Southeast Asia. He told us tales bursting with stabbings and shootings and fast cars and lots of people, with brutal big spenders and high stakes.

As he spoke, his eyes slid across the room, bored and wary. Tonight there would be no guns, no knives, no dangerous fortunes won or lost. Just a smattering of Mongolian import-export politicians with their bad suits and two-bit stakes and a handful of unsmiling Chinese traders, all business.

We tried to cheer him up, wracking our brains for instances of excitement and danger. Especially Brian, a competitive American and longtime Mongolia resident who could not bear to be outdone. 'Yeah, well, I've done some gambling here in UB,' he volunteered. Jacko looked at him expectantly. 'I shot hoops with some guys outside the Black Market. And once I tried that nut-in-a-cup thing.'

Jacko did not reply. In every way possible, Ulaanbaatar was the end of the line. There were few diversions for Jacko here. Not even the lissome Mongolian casino staff, whose company he enjoyed. 'If a casino manager tells you he's not fucking the staff,' said Jacko, 'he's lying.'

I felt for him. I really couldn't picture him doing the things most expats in Mongolia did. Getting drunk with a coven of consultants at the British Embassy's weekly booze-up, the Steppe Inn? Maybe, but he'd be bored. Cross-country skiing with UN programme officers? Peace Corps potlucks? It just wasn't going to happen.

Jacko spent his nights at the casino and his days, I assumed, in bed – first in the hotel, then in a flat in my building across the street. I never saw him outdoors. One day, after a couple of months, he just disappeared. I hope he went to a better place, where the gangsters have some flair, the girls at least rip you off, and everybody seems to know Jacko.

Chapter Nine

Sex on the Steppe

'This country is wild – it's like the sixties all over again!' said the Peace Corps volunteer, blond and beefy and flushed with lager and excitement. 'When Communism crumbled, the lid blew off.'

We were in the Top 10 nightclub, Ulaanbaatar's number-one purveyor of a hot night out. It was a large, high-ceilinged room with music loud enough and lighting dim enough to just about suggest a party palace – like a gymnasium transformed by strobe lights and a glitter ball for the weekly school disco. Around the perimeter, teenage boys stood nursing Cokes and watching teenage girls dance in a circle to Boney M's 'Brown Girl in the Ring.'

It wasn't exactly Studio 54.

My colleagues had assured me that nightclubs were *the* hot ticket in Ulaanbaatar. Every Saturday night all the girls in their crop tops and tight black jeans, all the boys in their shiny suits and gleaming leather shoes, squeezed onto trolleybuses or into the backs of Ladas, and headed off to the disco.

A decade earlier, in the waning days of the Communist regime, the author Nick Middleton had written a book called *The Last Disco in Outer Mongolia* – he'd found it, with some effort, in Ulaanbaatar's Bayangol Hotel. Now there were dozens of discos; all over town former shops, union halls and ground-floor flats were being converted with cheap chrome and fake marble.

Top 10 was the pick of the lot. It inhabited a broad concrete building near the railway station that looked like a 1970s council-estate community centre – which is basically what it was. It was a one-stop shop of modern entertainment options: a dark ground-floor bar; a bowling alley (two lanes, warped); kiosks and hot dog stands; and not one but two nightclubs.

One was the thrillingly high-concept (but, alas, always closed) Boeing 777, whose narrow interior had been fashioned to resemble a jet aeroplane, with curving walls and tiny oblong windows.

Top 10 was much larger, large enough to accommodate a mixed crowd of several hundred. It was dominated by teenagers, with a sprinkling of middle-aged couples in leather and fur, and a few families with children – the girls in their best dresses with bows in their hair, the boys in dark trousers and pressed white shirts.

The atmosphere was good-natured and noticeably less alcoholic than a typical bar. After forking out the equivalent of £2 to get in, the teenagers stuck to inexpensive Coke. A few groups of affluent businessmen sat at tables laden with bottles of vodka. Western consultants and aid workers sucked back imported lager.

The tinny sound system blasted out hardy disco perennials and a surprisingly large number of current Europop hits. (I know this because when they came on all the European expats whooped and rushed toward the dancefloor, while the North Americans looked at each other and muttered 'What is this shit?')

But the songs that really got the crowd going, the tunes you could be certain of hearing on a visit to any of the city's clubs, were Smokie's 'Living Next Door to Alice' ('Alice!? Who the fuck is Alice?'), and 'Rasputin' by Boney M. The latter would often be played two or three times, and at the line 'Oh, those Russians!' the Mongolians would collapse in hysterics.

Peace Corps Guy looked as delighted as if all 100 days of Sodom were unscrolling before him.

'The women here are great,' he said. 'They'll talk to you, they'll dance with you all night, and they might even go home with you if you buy them enough drinks.'

I noticed a couple of well-dressed young women laughing with two grizzled American oilmen at the bar. They could have been prostitutes or high-school pupils; it was impossible to tell.

'How can you tell if they're hookers?' I asked.

'Ah,' he said, 'There's a fine line between a hooker and a student.' And he waded into the crowd to become the centre of a dancing circle of girls.

Just before midnight, the thump and whine of the music suddenly stopped; everyone in the crowd drew back, stopped talking and looked expectantly toward the small stage. Slow music began to play. A thin young woman emerged, dressed in black and smoking a cigarette. She twirled and sashayed half-heartedly, languidly peeling off clothes before ending on a bravura note by doing the naked splits. Then the lights went dark and she scuttled off to polite applause. Everyone turned away and resumed chatting and dancing, the girls watching the boys and the boys watching the girls.

'What the hell was that?' I asked my Mongolian friends.

'Striptease,' explained Enkhtsetseg, patiently. 'It's very popular in Mongolia now,' she added. 'It's a new art form, a kind of dance.'

'It's a good way to make money, especially for students,' chipped in Chimgee.

I discovered that all the nightclubs in town offered almost exactly the same strip show, sometimes with a male bodybuilding display as an appetiser. A less erotic spectacle you can't imagine. No one seemed to regard it as such; it was accepted as a marker of sophistication, a sign of the new freedom – like *Hot Blanket* and the other soft-core titles on the news-stands, or like the elegantly dressed part-time hookers drumming their long nails on the tables of the city's hotel bars.

When I left Top 10, Peace Corps Guy was boogieing away to 'Daddy Cool,' a woman on each arm and a smile as wide as Wyoming on his face.

I thought later about what Peace Corps Guy had said. If this was a sexual revolution, it seemed a rather subdued one. Mongolians didn't talk much about sex.

But perhaps they didn't need to; there's no privacy in a *ger*, and not much in a cramped cold-water flat.

On one visit to a *ger*, I was awakened in the middle of the night by a robust chorus of grunts, creaks and moans from the other side of the tent. I lay holding my breath, rigid with embarrassment, but the other occupants snored on.

Mongolian children, it was explained to me, grow up in the countryside, seeing animals mate. Sex holds no mysteries for them. Teenage courtship tends to be a straightforward business. Even finding somewhere private to do the business is less difficult than I imagined. Many families have a spare storage *ger*, a sort of tool shed *ger*, to which lovers could slip away; and, in the summer at least, the whole vast steppe is your bedroom. Amorous couples would ride off across the steppe, dismount in some secluded spot, and stick an *urga* – a long pole with a lasso at the end – upright in the ground to warn passers-by not to come too close.

Not very romantic, I thought, but a healthy and pragmatic attitude. Mongolians seemed free of hang-ups about sex. I was particularly impressed by their artistic tradition of pastoral erotica. All over town, you could buy deft, expressive paintings showing traditionally-clad Mongolians coupling tantrically and athletically on horseback. On galloping horses. Upside down.

'Surely that's impossible?' I asked, squinting at an especially gymnastic feat on one of the postcards being sold outside the State Department Store. 'That woman would fall off the horse.'

The vendor looked offended. 'Mongolians,' he said, 'are very good horse-riders.'

Mongolians also seemed remarkably level-leaded about the consequences of sex. Mongolia, it's true, has a high teen-pregnancy rate, a pattern of early marriage and frequent divorce. But the combination of strong extended families and frequent periods of marital separation – husbands gone off to work in the city, or in Korea – had created a culture of stigma-free single parenthood and an unsentimental attitude toward adultery. A friend of mine once bumped into Mongolia's top pop diva at a temple; she'd come with her married boyfriend to seek the lama's blessing for their relationship. She got it.

The attitude to commercial sex appeared equally pragmatic. Year-round, the world's hardiest streetwalkers stood shivering in their miniskirts on the forecourt of the Ulaanbaatar Hotel; there was a small, pine-fringed park in front of the hotel, in the lee of Lenin's statue, seemingly designed for their purposes. Sharply-dressed, sleepy-eyed women hung around the bar of the Chinggis Khan Hotel, snuggling up to Chinese exporters and stray American oil prospectors. I was told there were even brothel *gers* in the suburbs, catering to visiting herders and truck drivers.

Prostitution was nominally illegal, and sometimes police would raid the brothels and march the hookers off to be tested for sexually transmitted diseases before letting them return to work. But there was little moral fuss about it; commentators more often lamented that economic necessity or economic temptation had driven so many women – mothers, teachers, students – into part-time prostitution.

In sex, as in so many things, Mongolians seemed determined to do things their own way. But Mongolians' belief in their own separateness made life difficult for some.

Sex education in schools was non-existent – considered a luxury when schools struggled to find books and pencils to teach Mongolian and maths. Most kids learned the facts of life in a rough-and-ready manner from gruff parental chats and observation of the livestock. For anything a bit out of the ordinary, they were on their own.

'I've never been to a country where there's *no* gay scene before,' marvelled Steve, a well-travelled expat friend. He'd spent six months in Mongolia without finding a single openly gay person – or even a closeted-but-self-aware gay person. He hadn't found them in the bars or nightclubs; he hadn't found them on the streets where young men unselfconsciously held hands and draped their arms around each other's shoulders; he hadn't even found them at the city's leading bodybuilding gym, where aspiring Mister Mongolias pumped iron and felt each other's sweaty muscles.

'Not even a seedy, clandestine scene,' he reported. 'Nothing. These are either the most repressed people in the world, or the most innocent.'

Gradually, we began to hear whispers of change. An American consultant said he'd heard you could pick up guys in a small park behind a block of flats near the State Department Store. Another said his buddy had gone home with a leggy hooker who turned out to be – well, a man.

Finally, we found the Five Star Disco Bar, a small, seedy dive that attracted barflies, hookers, the more daring expats and a smattering of proto-bohemian young Mongolians, including a few daring gay teenagers.

They were soft-spoken, polite and full of nervous bravado. No one was exactly sure whether homosexuality was illegal in Mongolia, but they said it was beyond the comprehension of most of their countrymen.

'Mongolians think all gay guys are like Gomo Naraa,' said one young man indignantly. Gomo Naraa was an infamous transvestite and petty criminal who lived by selling interviews to the tabloid press, threatening to expose high-level gomos – Russian for homosexuals – in politics and private life. He was Mongolia's only famous homosexual; the embodiment of homosexuality in the popular mind. 'And in the countryside it's even worse – they don't understand at all.'

They were nice kids. Infected by the new democratic spirit, they talked of setting up a gay club and a telephone helpline. We wished them well.

'Mongolia will get there in the end,' Steve said. 'But I think it's going to take a long, long time.'

Sometimes, Mongolians' robust faith in doing things their own way could mask a dangerous naivety. I was assured more than once that Mongolians could not get AIDS; the distinctive blood of the Mongolians offered immunity. Officially, the country had one of the lowest rates of HIV infection in the world: just a single confirmed AIDS patient, whose identity was a closely-guarded secret.

But there were worrying signs. Sexually transmitted

diseases were rife, and according to UNICEF between 50 and 80 per cent of cases went untreated. The government said half of those who were diagnosed were teenagers.

International agencies looked at the mounting AIDS toll in Mongolia's neighbours – economically booming China and economically devastated Russia – and told the government to prepare for the worst. The World Health Organisation said 100 Mongolians might be infected with HIV, maybe more. The country could not count on its legendary isolation.

It is, in any case, a lot less isolated than it likes to think. 'So many Mongolians go abroad for illegal work,' said Tsengelmaa, who helped run a women's centre in Ulaanbaatar. 'In Seoul all the Mongolians go to the brothels.' There were brothels, too, in the Chinese border towns that bustled with Mongolian traders, and a corps of Mongolian prostitutes in the hotels of Beijing.

The United Nations kicked into action. It sent government health officials to international conferences to learn from the experiences of other developing countries. Education, they were told, was the key to fighting AIDS. International agencies began to rain leaflets and condoms on Mongolia.

They met with a mixed response. 'Many rural Mongolians think condoms are for holding butter,' confided Tsogzolmaa, head of a group called the Women's Movement for Democracy. 'They can easily fit two kilograms of butter into one condom.'

Tsogzolmaa's group entered into the education campaign with gusto. Their motto: 'It is better to have sex with one person in many positions than many people in one position.' They reprinted images of horseback erotica to remind Mongolians of their proud heritage in this regard.

In some ways, the government also seemed receptive. It welcomed the condoms, and even seriously debated giving them to prison inmates. A civil servant and newspaper columnist called for brothels to be legalised and registered.

But some were still used to doing things differently. The UN had met with government leaders and urged them to take the threat of AIDS seriously. So the mayor of Ulaanbaatar issued a decree: all women between 18 and 40 would be tested for AIDS. Foreigners would also have to obtain a certificate attesting that they were HIV negative.

I was outraged. 'I'm not taking an AIDS test,' I said. 'It's a total infringement of my civil liberties.' I also knew they reused needles in Mongolian clinics; and I knew how high the hepatitis rate was.

As so often before, my colleagues seemed unperturbed. The UN, on the other hand, squirmed with embarrassment. Mongolia's newly democratic government, it seemed, retained Stalinist reflexes.

'It doesn't look good,' one diplomat told me. 'We've got Mongolia's first World AIDS Day event coming up, patting them on the back for recognising the power of education and information, and they're coming over like the Chinese government.

'At least the Chinese, if they said it, would do it. We've calculated how much it would cost to test a quarter of a million people for HIV; I don't think the Mongolian government has a spare $6 million sitting around.'

I thought the Mongolian Human Rights Committee might have something to say about the plan, but their leader, a man named Tsevegmid, was unperturbed. 'We can't consider this a human rights problem,' he told me. 'It's for the health of the women.'

In the end, authoritarianism was defeated by inefficiency. The authorities proposed to test 250,000 people in the space of two weeks, a big undertaking in any country. Anybody who gave it a moment's thought realised that the Mongolian government had neither the organisation nor the money to do such a thing.

The city's top health official, Terbish, said he was confident most women would volunteer to take the test; however, he said, the police had been authorised to assist local health authorities if any refused. (Terbish later accused the media of misrepresenting his position.)

Notices appeared in some health centres – but not in others – warning women they would be forced to take the test if they did not come voluntarily. There were scattered reports of police going door-to-door in blocks of flats. But I could not find a single woman who had been contacted, and no one I knew volunteered to be tested either.

Nonetheless, when the two weeks were up, the city's health officials announced that they had completed testing half of the targeted female population. (Under pressure from their UN benefactors, officials also said that the testing had been voluntary all along.) Soon the rest would be completed, and then testing would begin on men.

I never heard about the proposal again.

Neither the government nor the UN had been successful in making Mongolians feel that the AIDS crisis affected them. It took two fast-talking con men from Cameroon to do that.

The pair pitched up in Ulaanbaatar after travelling across Asia working their rudimentary scam. Among the trusting Mongolians, they must have thought they'd hit the jackpot. The swindle consisted of telling potential victims that they possessed a chemical that could triple the value of money; they'd demonstrate by inserting a dollar bill and extracting three. They showed the magic to some dealers at Ulaanbaatar's money-changing market. The dealers, mightily impressed, handed over US$30,000. The Cameroonians said such a large sum would take a little while to process; they would have to take the money away and would return two days later with $90,000. The dealers agreed.

The next day (better late than never), the Mongolian money-changers began to worry they'd made a mistake, and called the police. It didn't take much detective work to find where the two men were staying – an African in Ulaanbaatar is a head-turning rarity. Police arrived at the hotel just as the men were leaving to catch a plane to Beijing. Officers found the $30,000 in their socks.

The affair didn't do much for the reputation of Africans in Mongolia (it didn't do much for the reputation of Mongolian money-changers, either), but it got worse. In jail, the two men were tested for HIV, and one tested positive. He said he'd slept with four prostitutes while he was in Mongolia. The four were found; one of them also tested positive (although of course there was no way to know when she had become infected). She said she'd had sex with 12 Mongolian men since sleeping with the African.

This arithmetic lesson brought home the reality of AIDS like nothing else; people really began to worry. Prostitutes were rounded up and given tests for HIV and other STDs. The minister of health announced the prostitute's positive HIV test – which doubled the country's official AIDS toll – on national television. And he gave the nation some advice: 'You can protect yourselves and your families by avoiding excessive drinking and sleeping around,' he said.

It was hard to know what had been learned from the whole affair. After six weeks in prison, the Cameroonians were deported and the worry faded. AIDS was still considered a foreigners' disease.

At the same time, Mongolia remained a Western geek's paradise. No matter how homely or maladroit or married a guy had been at home, in Mongolia he – or possibly his passport – was a chick magnet.

The bars of Ulaanbaatar still offered up the sight of plump, middle-aged German agricultural consultants nestled among lithe young Mongolian women. The men wore expressions of utter delight. The women wore expressions of cautious hope. I think I know who was more likely to be disappointed.

Mongolia's first AIDS patient died in 1999. He was revealed as a 35-year-old railway engineer. He had been treated in secret for seven years; even his family had not known he had AIDS before his death.

Chapter Ten

Ghost Towns

On the map, Mongolia appears to have a liberal sprinkling of villages and towns – much as, on the map, it appears to be criss-crossed by roads. On the ground, there's Ulaanbaatar, and then there are ghost towns.

I've never felt more like an extra in a John Ford western than in Hatgal, a pretty little town set where the Eg River empties into majestic Lake Hovsgol.

I went there because – well, because nearly everyone who visits Mongolia goes to Hovsgol, an area the tourist brochures optimistically bill as 'the Switzerland of Central Asia.' I noted a distinct lack of chalets, but I wasn't disappointed by the scenery. Hovsgol is a big blue gash of a lake, more than 60 miles long, cupped in low pine-clad mountains on the Mongolian-Siberian border. It would be beautiful anywhere; in a stark, wind-blasted country of few trees and little water, it's spectacular. The lake itself is a stunning blue, ice cold, and so clear that it cries out to be bottled, labelled and sold for £2 a litre.

Several thousand foreign tourists – an absolute flood by Mongolian standards – visit the lake every year. They all have to pass through Hatgal. You'd think the town would be buzzing.

But when I arrived after a jarring 60-mile, five-hour jeep ride from the provincial capital, Moron (my all-time favourite place name), I found a sleepy, ramshackle village waiting for Wyatt Earp to turn up. Its single dusty street was lined with log cabins nestled under the pines;

horses were tethered to hitching posts outside. No one stirred. It was August, the height of Mongolia's short tourist season.

This, I learned when I stopped in on the local governor, was one of the poorest parts of the country. Togtokhnyam was a compact and energetic woman, one of the few female governors in the country. She told me the town's history, a typical tale of decline. A decade ago, the town had a population of 6,500 and a local industry based on logging and trade across the Russian border at the top of the lake. With the economic collapse of the 1990s, both businesses had withered. Now Hatgal had 2,800 residents and few jobs. Half the buildings in town stood abandoned and crumbling.

'The biggest problem here is unemployment,' Togtokhnyam told me. 'Living conditions are poor. People can't get money regularly, just some of the time. In wintertime, it's very difficult for me. My lobby is full of people asking for money, or food, or health care.'

She quoted me the Mongolian government's own depressing statistics – 64 per cent of Hatgal's population was classed as 'very poor' in 1997; 78 per cent of children under 18 were malnourished.

The situation was equally grim for many of Mongolia's provincial settlements, whose populations were shrinking as families and their livestock decamped for Ulaanbaatar's sprawling suburbs. These towns suffered from poor transportation and communication links, their industries were no longer 'economically viable,' there was no money for investment in infrastructure or industry, and local authorities received little support from the cash-strapped central government, which often couldn't afford to make the meagre transfer payments to the regions.

Many rural governors were famous for gobbling up the modest perks that went with their positions – the Russian jeep, the small bribes – and ignoring their constituents. But Togtokhnyam struck me as a savvy operator, an energetic advocate for her community who had learned to play the international-development game. She showed me her diary, full with visits: a delegation from the Japanese embassy, a group from UNICEF in town to do a workshop on iodine deficiency.

The governor said she sought help from international organisations because the central government, 500 miles away in Ulaanbaatar, was of little use. She was cannily aware that the village's postcard setting and relatively high profile gave it an edge over other deprived areas when it came to visits from foreign dignitaries.

But the international aid only went so far. The Japanese government had donated three generators to the town – but Hatgal was desperately short of the diesel needed to run them.

'We have to do everything ourselves, because the government is no help,' Togtokhnyam sighed. 'One of the things we need most here is electricity. What does the government tell us? That we should produce hydroelectric power! But of course nothing is being done.

'Our problem is that we have a poor and uneducated population. There is high unemployment, and it is a long way to hospitals and other services. We really need to develop schools and health care.'

If the state of health care is a measure of a region's vitality, then the prognosis for Hatgal was bleak. In the village, I met Orna, an Irish nurse, and Tigi, a Mongolian doctor. They had travelled from Ulaanbaatar to visit women in Hatgal and the surrounding countryside.

'We're seeing very high incidences of malnutrition, anaemia, and sexually transmitted diseases,' Orna told me – though, without laboratory facilities, she admitted, many conditions were hard to diagnose.

Even when diagnosis was possible, treatment often was not. Orna said the local hospital lacked the most basic medicines, such as antibiotics and even aspirin. She and Tigi quickly exhausted the supply they'd brought from the city. When they encountered a patient whom they were pretty sure had tuberculosis, all they could tell her was to eat well and get plenty of rest. They knew there was slim chance even of that.

The local hospital, a one-storey wooden structure, was still functioning, barely. When I went there one evening, the rooms were musty, dark and all but empty. One dusky chamber held a rail-thin, coughing man on a cot and nothing else. 'He's dying,' whispered Tigi, as we hovered in the doorway.

In another room, a doctor and a nurse were attending a 40-year-old woman in labour. 'I hope she gives birth before it gets dark,' said the nurse cheerfully, 'because there's no electricity.' In a corner of the delivery room was a shiny new incubator – another gift from the generous Japanese. It had never been used.

All this was fairly typical of a small Mongolian town. But why, I asked the governor, did Hatgal – the largest settlement within Lake Hovsgol National Park – see so little profit from the tourist trade?

She said most visitors came as part of organised tour groups and bypassed the town to stay at privately owned *ger* camps up the lake. It's not that the town wasn't trying. With the help of a couple of enthusiastic US Peace Corps volunteers, residents had set up a shiny new park visitors' centre on the outskirts of the village. Only 1,000 tourists had stopped by all summer.

But, Togtokhnyam went on, they were still doing their best to get a piece of the tourism pie. The town had set up its own high-end lakeside *ger* camp in an attempt to bring tourist dollars into the community. In Hatgal itself, there was the Blue Pearl Hotel, a (surprise!) log cabin structure offering cheap, clean rooms to foreign travellers. There was also a local crafts collective and shop. 'We're hoping tourism can bring money into the area,' said Togtokhnyam. She did not sound desperately optimistic.

All Mongolian provincial towns have a similar eerie air. Perhaps they were always so, even before the economic collapse of the past decade; as a nomadic culture, Mongolia has little history of large settlements. When the country fell into the Soviet orbit, towns were thrown up quickly and cheaply. They are Communism's company towns, designed to be administrative centres – though relatively little administration goes on now – and built around some now-crumbling mine or mill or factory. I suspect that, like so many postwar large-scale building projects (in the West too), they began to look rundown almost as soon as they were completed.

Perhaps it's the country's nomadic soul asserting itself, but Mongolian towns have an air of impermanence. The first time I travelled outside of Ulaanbaatar, driving through a series of *soum* centres, the equivalent of county towns, on my way to the Gobi desert, I was puzzled by a feeling of familiarity. It took me a while to figure out what these settlements, with their unpaved streets and rows of *gers* in wooden enclosures, put me in mind of. There was something *suburban* about them. They sprawled; no building was more than one storey tall, and the construction materials were cheap. Then there were the *gers*, nomads' homes unnaturally rooted within fenced compounds. That was it: they reminded me of a trailer park.

Even more depressing are the abandoned military bases that dot the countryside. Once there were 100,000 Soviet troops stationed in Mongolia. They pulled out rapidly, within a couple of years, leaving behind huge complexes of buildings that were quickly stripped to skeletons, as local Mongolians – resentful or resourceful – carted away wood and metal and brick, windows and doors and lamp posts. (Someone who worked at Baganuur, a coal-mining town and the site of one of the Russian bases, told me how the Russians had deliberately destroyed all the equipment they could before they left so the Mongolians wouldn't be able to use it.) Other families moved into the drafty, windowless hulks. Towns such as Choir, along the Trans-Mongolian railway line, became squatters' communities.

Even Ulaanbaatar has a transient air. After the Mongol Empire collapsed, it was several hundred years before the divided and demoralised Mongols founded a new national capital. They moved its location several times before settling on its present site in the Tuul River valley at the end of the eighteenth century. At the time of the 1921 revolution, it consisted of little more than *gers*, Gandan Monastery and the wooden palace of the Bogd Khan.

But there is one town in Mongolia that can claim a glorious past if not an affluent present: Kharkhorin. Not that you'd notice straight away. The first thing I noticed is that Kharkhorin is not exactly the shopping capital of Central Asia. It was the summer Naadam holiday, and my friends had sent me into town from our riverside campsite half a mile away in search of bread. A ramble through the grid of dusty, unpaved streets, crumbling blocks of flats, and tattered *gers* behind sagging fences turned up an outdoor market – myriad cheap Chinese toys, children's clothes and jars of pickles, but no bread – and three desultory shops. The first sold potatoes and lumpy yogurt in dirty green bottles. The second was closed. The third – potatoes, pickles and (aha!) a single loaf of bread. I reached for it. 'Don't bother,' said the woman behind the counter, twitching one eye up from her two-week-old newspaper. 'It's bad.'

At first glance – oh, let's face it, at any glance – Kharkhorin looks like any other small Mongolian town. It's a dump. As I shuffled along its pitted streets, walking past the idle flour mill and stopping in the dusty sepia square to have my picture taken in front of a rusting statue of a tractor, I didn't find it difficult to imagine this as the centre of the largest land empire the world has ever known. I found it impossible.

But this scattering of dust and horses in the valley of the Orkhon River was once the stuff of legend. It was here, in 1220, that Chinggis Khan decided to knuckle under and build a permanent capital for his expanding empire: Karakorum.

When the Franciscan friar William of Rubruck visited Karakorum in 1254, he described a compact, cosmopolitan community swarming with traders, missionaries and emissaries from many lands. There were Buddhist temples and mosques, Christian priests and entranced shamans. There was a vast royal pavilion – the palace of Tumen Amgalant, Infinite Tranquillity – with a splendid silver fountain in the shape of a tree, its serpent-head branches spewing wine, fermented mare's milk, mead and rice wine for the khan's guests. Almost against his will – it was, he complained, rather a small town – William was impressed.

Well, he wouldn't recognise the place today. By the 1260s, Chinggis' grandson Khubilai Khan had moved the imperial capital to Beijing, beginning Mongolia's drift, first to the periphery of its own empire, then to the fringes of the world's consciousness.

Left to crumble, fought through and around by Mongol tribes, razed by Manchu soldiers, and, in the 1950s, bulldozed under a state farm, ancient Karakorum has been almost completely erased. Two stone markers in the shape of turtles that once guarded the city gates are all that remain.

One of the biggest culprits is the modern town's sole redeeming feature: the huge monastery of Erdene Zuu (One Hundred Treasures). It was commissioned in the sixteenth century by Avtai Khan, ruler of a few remaining scraps of the Mongol Empire, and built from whatever remained of old Karakorum. And it was built to impress. Its sweeping whitewashed walls, each nearly 440 yards long, are studded with 108 stupas. At its peak, it housed 60 temples and 10,000 lamas.

It's still an impressive structure. It does get your hopes up, though. As our jeep rattled toward Kharkhorin after a jarring eight-hour drive from Ulaanbaatar, we saw it from miles away, at the centre of the broad valley: a ship afloat on the billowing green steppe, its stupas brilliant in the afternoon sunlight.

Inside the enormous walls are a handful of cool, aromatic temples and acres of grass (and a gift shop). Erdene Zuu today has a soothing sense of space that its builders never intended. Once it must have been a tightly packed compound swarming with brightly robed monks. But most of the buildings were knocked down in the terrifyingly thorough Stalinist purges of the 1930s. Many of the monks were shot.

Today Erdene Zuu is Kharkhorin's only tourist attraction. But that doesn't stop local residents from dreaming of the day their town is restored to its ancient glory. Like the rest of Mongolia, Kharkhorin is down, but it's not out.

A group of parliamentarians recently tabled a motion

to move the capital of Mongolia from Ulaanbaatar – population 650,000 and growing – to Kharkhorin, population 20,000 and shrinking. The proposal raised a few smiles in Ulaanbaatar. But no one laughed. Indeed, the government took the idea seriously enough to strike a committee, including several high-profile MPs, the president of the Mongolian Academy of Sciences, and the head of the National University, to study the idea.

And the notion has struck a chord among Mongolians disoriented by the country's head-spinning 1990s transition from obscure communist outpost to struggling capitalist state. Mongolians are proud of their imperial past, however distant it may now seem, and fiercely determined – in the language absorbed during 70 years of Communism – to 'develop' their homeland. In the minds of some, the idea for a new capital is a brilliant fusion of the two – a world-class historical heritage site crossed with a gleaming Brasilia of the steppe.

The secretary of the parliamentary working group, D. Khoroldambaa, described his vision to a Mongolian newspaper reporter. The reconstructed Palace of Infinite Tranquillity would be the seat of the national government. Tourists would flock to see the restored glories of Karakorum. The new city would promote regional development and relieve pressure on polluted, overcrowded Ulaanbaatar.

'This has been the site of Mongolian capitals for most of the past 2,000 years,' he said. 'It's located smack in the centre of Mongolia, in the middle of the Altai-Khangai mountain chain and at the confluence of the

143

forest, steppe and desert regions of the country. It's set in a broad, fertile valley, far less prone than Ulaanbaatar to air pollution.'

And – here he delivered the *coup de grâce* of his argument – if the Kazakhs could move their capital, forsaking bustling Almaty for remote Astana, so could the Mongolians.

Much to my surprise, I never met a Mongolian who was prepared, like me, to laugh the idea off as a crackpot scheme. 'New York isn't the capital of America, is it?' said a co-worker. 'It's Washington, a much smaller town.' That was true, I admitted, but where on earth was the money going to come from to turn Kharkhorin into a seat of government? My colleague lowered his voice a fraction. 'We hope the Japanese will pay for it,' he said.

In Kharkhorin itself, I discovered, the scheme is not viewed as crazy at all. As I was relaxing at the campsite one day – alternately soaking in the fast-flowing river and dozing on the grass – I spotted two men on horseback riding toward me across the plain. One was European, caked in dust and wearing a traditional Mongolian robe. The other was a Mongolian, nattily dressed in chinos and a black turtleneck.

The European was a Frenchman named Benoit whom I'd met a couple of times in Ulaanbaatar in the company of a chatterbox, mobile-phone-toting attaché from the French Embassy. Benoit was on an extended solo horse trek across Mongolia – the sort of nutty plan that seems to seize every second foreigner who goes there.

Benoit was having a bad week. He'd arrived in

Kharkhorin a few days earlier, two weeks out of Ulaanbaatar, and camped by the river, near where we were now. When he woke up in the morning, his horse was gone. He was sold another mount by a local who'd befriended him, but this horse, it was obvious even to me, was on the verge of death. Benoit flailed desperately in an attempt to get it up to a trot, but the horse was stubborn. Benoit had the look of a man who realises he has made a bad deal but knows there is no way out. (Two nights later, Benoit 'forgot' to hobble the horse, and it waded across the river and ran away. He looked more relieved than upset.)

Benoit's friend was a local man who was helping him look for his lost horse. He was deaf and mute, but he and Benoit had developed an extraordinary ability to communicate via an improvised sign language. We managed some rudimentary introductions and greetings. Then the man made a flurry of gestures in the direction of Benoit, who nodded.

'He says,' Benoit translated, 'that Kharkhorin may not look like much now, but in a few years you won't recognise it. It'll be bigger and more important than Ulaanbaatar once they finish paving the road. There will be cars everywhere.'

I just stared at Benoit.

'Well, that's what he said,' he shrugged.

Mongolians, I thought. Stoic survivors – but dreamers still.

Chapter Eleven

The King of the Tabloids

In a street just off Ulaanbaatar's central Sukhbaatar Square stands a glass case containing one of those newspaper boards that were such a prominent feature of communist countries (capitalist countries being loath to give daily newspapers away for free). Tacked inside is the day's edition of Mongolia's official communist newspaper, *Truth*. I used to walk down this street frequently, and there would usually be one or two people peering through the glass, absorbing the party's take on the day's events.

Then I'd round a corner and there'd be dozens of people elbowing for space around one of the tables that served as newspaper kiosks at street corners and bus stops. These ubiquitous stalls were spread thick with newspapers, from colourful tabloids to staid broadsheets. *Truth* – for decades the country's only daily newspaper – was in there, but no one ever bought it. The people were more likely to be reaching for 'THE BIGGEST TITS IN MONGOLIA' (with photos that made a compelling case) or 'I WAS THE PRESIDENT'S MISTRESS,' for papers with titles such as *Alarm Clock*, *Top Secret* and *Disgusting Crimes*. I'd never seen a country that had embraced freedom of the press with such speed and enthusiasm.

In 1999, the Ministry of Justice listed more than 800 registered newspapers. To be sure, many appeared sporadically if at all. But dozens hit the streets regularly every week or ten days, in a blaze of garish colour, screaming headlines, and, often, a flamboyant disregard for evidence or probity.

Even the names were gloriously unrestrained, ranging from the pedestrian (*Today*) to the touchingly honest (*Yesterday*) to the downright reckless (*The Day after Tomorrow*). They were a heady mix of showbiz news and gossip, political rumour, lurid crime stories and anything to do with sex. Many threw in topless or nude photos to spice up the mix. Articles ranged from social comment ('TEENS GO INSANE AFTER ATTENDING CHRISTIAN MEETING') to human-interest tragedy ('YOUNGSTER BLINDED IN BASKETBALL MISHAP') to a combination of both ('MOTHER KILLED HER BABY BECAUSE LAMA TOLD HER TO').

These papers were always in trouble, slinging political dirt and celebrity innuendo, being denounced in parliament, getting hauled into court and threatened with censure. But they carried on, and people carried on reading them.

If anyone could be called the father of the tabloid press in Mongolia, it was Bayarmonkh, the editor of *Alarm Clock*, which in 1998 surpassed the government-owned daily *People's Right* to become the nation's bestselling newspaper.

Nothing in the standard-issue first half of Bayarmonkh's CV suggested a populist media pioneer. He was a graduate of the Lvov Military and Political Academy who started his career in journalism on the party-approved military newspaper *Red Star*. But in 1993 he became the founding editor of *Hot Blanket*, the first and most legendary of Mongolia's independent papers.

When I went to see Bayarmonkh in his spartan office on the ground floor of an Ulaanbaatar block of flats, I met a stocky, affable man in his mid-thirties who oozed contentment with himself and his role.

'When I was working at *Red Star*, society was in motion,' he told me with his disarming smile. 'Everyone was doing business, trading and making money. I've no talent for trade. So I tried to think of something I could do.'

He soon stumbled onto a talent that would serve him better than he could have imagined – a knack for tweaking the zeitgeist of a society wracked by convulsive change. The vehicle of his epiphany was a set of dirty playing cards.

'At the time, I had these cards with pictures of naked women on the back,' he said warmly. 'I started noticing that all my friends were extremely interested in them. One time this big official asked to look at them and took them for two or three days. That's when I had the idea for an erotic newspaper.'

The result of this brainwave was *Hot Blanket*, a cheaply produced paper with rough newsprint, blotchy photos of naked Bulgarian women and an inspired title. It was a sensation.

'The first street vendor I took it to refused to sell it,' said Bayarmonkh with the chuckle of the vindicated. 'We needed to sell a copy for three tugrug to make a profit. We sold it for 15, and there were even some people buying it for 15 and selling it for 25 on the black market. We sold 80,000 copies an issue. Soon that first vendor came to me, begging for copies.'

The government pulled the plug on *Hot Blanket* in 1996. But by that time Bayarmonkh had already moved on, sensing that readers were losing interest in the crude thrill of low-rent erotica. He had other crude thrills in mind.

'I realised,' he told me, 'that it's better to have a paper addressing broad social and economic issues.'

The paper of his dreams was *Alarm Clock*, a canny mix of celebrity gossip, scandal and muckraking political exposé. Bayarmonkh had an instinctive tabloid sense, a knack for spotting – and stealing – explosive stories. He pioneered the cut-throat tactics of tabloid competition in a nation steeped in 'the commissar says' journalism.

'If you want to succeed in newspapers,' he told me, 'you have to understand social psychology. *Alarm Clock* seizes opportune moments, when something happens in society. We reveal the secret lives of famous people, and that attracts people's attention.'

Later he put it a little more crudely. 'I scooped the exclusive interview with the father of pop diva Sarantuya's child,' he boasted. 'It was easy – I was the only editor willing to pay a million tugrug for the story.'

Bayarmonkh had a real flair for attention-grabbing stunts. Several years earlier, he'd flown the cast of an immensely popular Venezuelan soap opera to Mongolia. People were still talking about it.

All this had not exactly made Bayarmonkh the most popular man in Mongolia. Many people despised the crude new force he represented. Politicians, for a start, who routinely found themselves the subject of his sensational splashes, condemned Bayarmonkh and other practitioners of the 'yellow press' (the literal Mongolian term – there is even a newspaper called *Yellow News*) for, variously, scandal-mongering, inaccuracy, a lack of professionalism and an absence of social responsibility.

It's a hard case to answer, and Bayarmonkh didn't really try, preferring to adopt the role of the rakish, arrogant tabloid editor. He once told a foreign reporter that he preferred hiring untrained novices to write for his paper. Professionals had the nasty habit of getting their own ideas and not doing what he said.

He also argued, with some justification, that politicians are afraid of a free press. 'Independent newspapers have the freedom to publish whatever we want,' he told me. 'No one can dictate to us. We can reveal corruption and scandals related to members of the government. Then the officials organise a press conference to deny it – and the government media report their denials. I have a lot of enemies,' he said, folding his hands on his desk. 'And a lot of friends.'

It often felt like there was a war being waged in, and for, the Mongolian media. Politicians hurled multimillion tugrug lawsuits at newspapers; they dragged on, reported in hyperbolic detail. No one ever seemed to have to pay. Pro and anti-government newspapers denounced each other, histrionically. The presses roiled with the financial shenanigans and lurid misdeeds of the political, economic and criminal elite (often one and the same). Crimes were recounted in gruesome, graphic detail. It all made for gloriously unhinged reading. Mongolians, who had never encountered anything like it, read on, aghast and enthralled. It sold newspapers.

It also had consequences. One evening in April 1999, a 21-year-old cub reporter for *Alarm Clock* named Munkhbayasgalan stepped out of the office (she recounted later) to buy coffee from a kiosk. In the dark entranceway to the building, she was grabbed by a masked man, who pinned her arms down as he slashed at her face with a sharp blade, like a razor.

Munkhbayasgalan and her scars were paraded on television and in the papers; Mongolia's media put on as fine a show of self-righteousness as any in the world. *Alarm Clock*, and word on the street, were quick to point the finger of blame.

Alarm Clock had lately been running a typically lurid series of stories involving a member of parliament. Dashbalbar, the lone parliamentary representative of the Mongolian Traditional United Party, was the country's most vocal ultranationalist – a sort of Mongolian Zhirinovsky. A well-known poet with a passion for grandiose oratory, a fondness for paramilitary uniforms, and a shining mane of black hair, he loved to denounce the government, American influence and the Chinese; he had been known to praise Saddam Hussein and Hitler.

Dashbalbar was a marginal political figure – his party was in no danger of winning power or even of electing another MP – but a popular one. His love of country and his way with language were unquestioned; he could always be relied upon for a colourful quote or an entertaining speech.

But *Alarm Clock* had sinister allegations to make. Munkhbayasgalan claimed that, during a holiday-season party attended by Dashbalbar and his friends, the MP had confined her to a room and attempted to sexually assault her. She also said – a bizarre and macabre twist, this – that he had cut his own hand and tried to make her drink his blood.

Dashbalbar denied all the charges, but the paper was convinced the story and the attack on its reporter were connected. The whole sordid saga became a sensation in all the papers. Dashbalbar resorted to showing his hands (scar free) to reporters, while newspapers friendly to the MP (or unfriendly to *Alarm Clock*) claimed Munkhbayasgalan had fabricated the story of the attack. Her colleagues swore she was telling the truth.

It was a gripping display, and it shifted a lot of papers. But I couldn't help thinking that people were getting hurt here, and I wasn't quite sure who. The naive young reporter? The bullish MP? Dashbalbar died later the same year of liver disease, so the truth may never be known.

In any event, amid the burgeoning freedom was a reckless inexperience that often ran roughshod over the truth. The rule of law had not yet hardened; libel trials were common, but they dragged on and on as one court overruled another's decision.

And, for all the show of anarchy, the newspapers still operated on rigidly partisan lines. The state-owned *People's Right* and *Government News* supported the government; the private daily *Today*, whose owner had worked for the government press before the election of the Democrats, favoured the opposition Communists. The tabloids – well, they were independent, so that meant against the government. The words *fair* and *balanced* didn't really enter into it.

New, embryonic notions of independent reporting nestled column-to-column with the old, Soviet-schooled style of journalism. Both used to drive me crazy when I started to work at the *UB Post*. Each day I'd ask my reporters to fill me in on what was in the day's press. The stories were generally of two kinds. On government decisions, political debates and so on, the papers would print the speeches of the major players involved. The whole speeches, often spilling over two or even three pages. The reporters would volunteer to translate the whole thing for inclusion in the *Post*.

'There's no need,' I'd say. 'Just summarise the decisions, pick out a couple of the best quotes from the speeches, and we'll work from there.'

I was met with anxious looks. They were unused to having to find an angle for a story or extract the most compelling information.

The other type of story consisted of small items, often of only a couple of paragraphs, recounting the most sensational, compelling tidbits of information. An earthquake has struck Mongolia. The prime minister will resign today. That sort of thing. I'd get really excited over these stories.

'What? The police have arrested a cabinet minister

for booze smuggling and murder? When? Where is he being held?'

'It doesn't say.'

'Well, what source is given in the paper?'

'Um . . . "a reliable source."'

'Well, phone the police and check it out.'

The story would always prove to be completely unsubstantiated.

In the end, we managed. The reporters learned to read both government and anti-government press and search down the middle for the truth, to filter the nuggets of fact from the slew of conjecture and opinion. In time, they even began to phone sources in authority for confirmation and quotes, though this was a major hurdle. Many Mongolians, even the young, retain a deep deference for authority – indeed for anyone who is old – and a reluctance to talk back.

(This is not altogether a bad quality, particularly in regard to respect for the elderly. At the same time, I found that Mongolians in positions of power were amazingly candid in interviews, often to their own cost. They had yet to learn the power of spin.)

One side effect of this deference is that Mongolians – who, it has been pointed out, have relied heavily on the advice of 'foreign advisors' in affairs of state since the time of the Mongol Empire – treat the opinions of foreigners with the utmost respect. Or at least they give that impression. The result is that the foreigner, no matter how incompetent, often becomes something of a star.

This is as true of the media as of the government.

My friend Chris – who, I hasten to point out, is not at all incompetent – was sent by an Australian volunteer organisation to work on the Voice of Mongolia, the country's English-language shortwave radio service. He found himself in an office in the echoing labyrinth of Mongol Radio and Television, a brutalist monstrosity that loomed over a *ger* district in the city's northern suburbs. He was one of a four-member team producing five half-hour programmes a week, and he was desperately bored.

So he asked for his own show on domestic radio. And he got it. An hour on Tuesday afternoons to play records from the station's disco-heavy collection and blather in English – for a potential audience in the tens – with two other expats, Dave and Mike (and sometimes, I admit, me). It was called the Short, Grey and Curly hour, ostensibly in reference to the hosts' hairstyles. It was mildly diverting if you were actually in the studio with them. I can't imagine it travelled well. The highlight of the show was a phone-in, during which, in the show's year-long run, only five people ever called.

Nonetheless, Chris soon found out that the station was repeating the broadcast – in prime time – later in the week. Sometimes twice.

And his celebrity didn't end there. He also had another common experience for expats in Mongolia. He was asked to appear in a TV commercial. He played a picky customer purchasing a brand of holiday biscuit-bread. Its name was his only line. For the day-long shoot, he was paid the princely sum of 5,000 tugrug, about £3.50; he didn't even get to keep the bread. But he was briefly a celebrity, pointed at in bars and hailed by taxi drivers. When he eventually left Mongolia, he was recognised with back-slapping glee by fellow passengers on the train to Beijing.

The tabloid assault did much to undermine Mongolians' faith in figures of authority and in the press itself. It was a trend that worried many people. Enkhtuya, one of the new generation of 'modernising' Democrat MPs, told me her constituents frequently voiced their anxiety.

'When I go to my district, people ask me to shut down newspapers,' she said. 'They say, "We don't believe anyone anymore." The Mongolian people are not used to having many sources of information. They always believed there should be one source of true information. It's the mentality. And the tendency of the Mongolian paparazzi to become very strong and dominate public opinion doesn't just make it hard for the government and parliament to operate; it creates a mistrustful atmosphere in the whole society. People start not believing any information.'

Enkhtuya was one of a group of MPs attempting to push a new press-freedom law through parliament. That was its name, the Press-Freedom Law – and, indeed, it was designed to enshrine the independence of the media and ban state ownership of the press. But it was equally about reining in journalists.

The politicians did not enjoy being the villains of a hundred grubby sheets. And they despaired, amid the reigning chaos, of ever winning redress from newspapers that had wronged them.

'Our main problem,' Enkhtuya said with a sigh, 'is that we have a very low level of journalism in Mongolia. Many people understand freedom of expression to mean that anybody can say what they want, write what they want. It's democracy after a totalitarian system, but that's why there is no clear understanding of this term. It's a difficult process.

'Formally, we have libel laws. Everybody has the right to go to court if somebody has written lies about them. But there are a lot of difficulties in exercising this right. We have formally independent courts, but they have no experience in this field, no knowledge about it.

'And there is a lot of political manipulation, because the political struggle between old and new is very strong here right now. The population is very polarised. Many people use this situation to make political gains. It's a very dangerous process which is going on in the Mongolian mass media.'

The independent papers, for their part, were no angels, but they did have a point. They argued, with some justification, that the state-owned papers had privileged access to government officials and official information and to a subsidised national distribution network that gave them an unfair circulation advantage.

Government and journalists alike agreed that the first step toward solving the problem was the separation of media and state. A working group was struck to thrash out the details of the privatisation plan; foreign consultants were brought in to advise. I went along to one of their sessions, where a well-spoken Canadian journalist and a Hungarian lawyer were explaining to

Mongolian editors how an independent press should operate.

They were running through the notion of a government press office. The government could issue press releases, details of its bills, reports and so on to *all* media outlets, and the media could do what they liked with the information. Any questions?

One woman put up her hand. 'So, does the government pay us for publishing the information, or do we pay them?'

Clearly this was not going to be easy. In the end, it was a disaster. The consultants went home disillusioned, and the working group kept delaying its recommendations. The 1 January deadline for privatisation came, and it was declared that the state-owned newspapers were now independent (no one even wanted to mention the flat-broke behemoth of Mongol Radio and Television). But they kept on publishing, out of the same offices and on the same equipment, only they changed their names, so that *Government News* became the much catchier *News of the Century*, and *People's Right* shed names like sheets of paper, running through (within a month*)* *National People's Right*, *National Right*, the *Daily Mirror* (my favourite; I wanted them to stop there), and finally the *Daily News*.

Their rivals cried foul and headed for the courts. It was a mess. And it still is.

Many Mongolians may have despaired at the scandalous state of their media, but others revelled in the new freedom. Editors like Bayarmonkh found themselves masters of public opinion. Sophisticates such as Ganbold found they could at last engage with the bright wired world.

Ganbold was a suave and cosmopolitan man in his forties, a former member of one of Mongolia's leading 1980s pop bands, who now produced the *E-Mail Daily News*, an electronic digest of Mongolian news in English that he sold to a subscriber base of news-starved expats and dedicated Mongolists.

(I say in English, but it was actually in educated Monglish, a delightful combination of English vocabulary and Russian grammar. 'Heated was the debate in parliament today . . .' a typical item would begin. It was like reading a 1940s newsreel.)

Ganbold spoke perfect English. I met him in his flat, in a typical low-rise block granted prestige by its central Peace Avenue location and allegedly superior Chinese construction. Ganbold's flat was atypically modernist: bright, airy, the walls adorned with colourful modern Mongolian art, of which he was a serious collector. One or two pieces of furniture even looked as if they might have come from IKEA.

Ganbold read English newspapers and subscribed to the *Far Eastern Economic Review*. He was sanguine about the chaotic state of the Mongolian press.

'There was a time in this country when you were supposed to present social life within the limits of one model,' he said. 'You can imagine that, after several decades of being strangled by laws and regulations and orders, one can feel very happy that you are entitled to do whatever you want.

'It was boiling too long. Now we've taken the lid off the saucepan, and the steam is pouring out.'

Ganbold was confident that, with time, things would settle down. 'The problem is, Mongolia is too far away from the rest of the world. It remains isolated in an information sense. What we need is to introduce more new technology and make it more accessible for readers, viewers, and people from abroad who are interested in Mongolia. We need to bring Mongolia closer to the rest of the world.'

Enkhtuya was not so sure. 'In 1990, when the reforms started, we suddenly had lots of newspapers. And everybody was happy, because at this time there was no free information. There was so much secret information that there was a boom of information. Everybody wanted to know. It was an explosion. And now I think the public is ready not to accept such a bad quality of information. Many in the electorate are saying they don't want such information, just about crime. In the past, it was not allowed to write detailed reports about crime. Now everybody writes only about crime.

'Pornography was prohibited shortly after the last election, and it created some problems with the journalists. They said the government was acting against freedom of the press. That's how people understand freedom of the press. They say it's a human-rights issue. They don't think that getting true information is a human-rights issue too. Now we have the balance in favour of journalists. That's why the public is concerned about the danger.'

She, too, made it sound a bit like a war.

Bayarmonkh would have agreed with her. He spoke of the government – which included an old *Red Star* colleague, now the prime minister – as an intractable enemy. 'The government is trying to destroy us. That's their policy,' he told me. 'My philosophy is, in order to be a good editor, I have to have money. I have to be ready, and I have to have a plan.

'You know, I'm a simple man,' he said absently. 'All my attention is focused on my newspaper. My wife's always after me to polish my shoes or get a haircut, but I'm always busy. I don't care about money for myself; it's all for the paper.'

He gazed out at his car, a green Mercedes, parked in the forecourt. He caught me following his glance. 'It's a 1982 model!' he exclaimed.

Chapter Twelve

A Hearty Meal

It's all true. One of the Mongolian tourist industry's proudest boasts – along with the vast open spaces, the yaks, the Buddhist temples – is the hospitality of the country's traditionally nomadic people.

A trip to the Mongolian countryside will not disappoint. Approaching a *ger*, no Mongolian would think of knocking at the door – though a preemptive shout of 'Call off your dog!' is advised. Just push open the door and march in; feel the glow of smoky warmth radiating out from the iron stove – fuelled by coal or wood or, in poorer, remoter homes, by animal dung – and inhale the archetypal scent of Mongolia: essence of boiled mutton, sour milk and cheap Bulgarian cigarettes.

(This smell, which even pervades the banknotes, seeps into the visitor as well. You may not notice until you sense the odd looks you're getting from people in the airport when you arrive home and see them discreetly backing away.)

As a guest in a *ger*, you will be invited to take a seat by the stove and plied with tea and food. If you are foreign, you will find your hosts friendly but reserved, curious but unimpressed. They'll be keen to know about the weather in your country and how many livestock there are (a statistic not on the tips of most Westerners' tongues, strangely enough – look it up before you leave home).

You can stay and chat as long as you like without being

asked to leave, and if night falls you will be offered a place to sleep on the floor or – more likely, as you are a guest – on one of the two or three beds that the family shares.

And when you leave, your hosts will think it odd and find it a bit embarrassing if you offer thanks – though you are expected to quietly slip the head of the household a small gift, such as some candles or matches or vodka or cigarettes.

It's an experience of natural, unforced hospitality that no traveller will ever forget.

But I'll let you in on a secret: there's not a foreign resident in Mongolia who hasn't secretly dreaded that famous nomad hospitality just a little. And I'll tell you why. It's the food. The essence of the Mongolian diet can be captured in one word: mutton.

I went for three decades without eating mutton once; in Mongolia it is difficult to go a day without eating some. A country of 2.5 million people has 15 million sheep and a grindingly unvarying diet: boiled mutton with rice, boiled mutton with noodles, boiled mutton in a dumpling.

Mongolians have what my Lonely Planet guidebook dryly referred to as 'one of the world's most rudimentary cuisines.' Nonetheless, food is central to family life, hospitality and celebrations, and even such a basic diet tells a fascinating story.

Take the mania for mutton. Mongolia's climate of extremes makes agriculture difficult, and in any case Mongolians have a nomad's antipathy to settling down and cultivating the land. Their diet, as a result, is based almost exclusively on what animals can provide: dairy products and meat. (These, with vodka, may be considered the major food groups of the Mongolian diet.)

This is one of the few countries on earth in which meat is not a luxury but a staple, the very staff of life. Many Mongolians greet the notion of vegetarianism with blank incomprehension. What else is there to eat?

A simple Mongolian meal – and really there is no other kind – tells a great deal about the country's culture and its history, as I discovered one day in a *ger* when I asked my hostess, Bolormaa, about the food she was serving to her guests.

She was happy to describe it, if a bit surprised that such a simple act of hospitality should need explanation. 'First I'll offer everyone a bowl of *suutei tsai* and some *aaruul*,' she said, 'and then I'll get to work on making the *buuz*.'

Suutei tsai is Mongolian tea; the Mongolians are as passionate about tea as the English, gulping down litres of the stuff each day. Bolormaa showed me how Mongolians brew up – by boiling together in a large pot water, milk, a handful of tea chipped off a pressed block and a dash of salt.

It is rather an acquired taste. As tea, it is extremely weak; the fresh milk adds a musky flavour; and the drink is salty, which kind of defeats the whole purpose of a beverage, if you ask me.

But there's the whole story of Mongolia in that pot: the herder's staple drink, milk, mixed with tea, which was introduced from China in the days of the Mongol

Empire. The Mongols acquired a taste for the drink, and it stuck. The tea they use – tea bricks, a cut-price combination of the cheapest leaves and a large number of stems – speaks of the country's poverty.

Bolormaa ladled out bowls of tea for her guests – who slurped appreciatively – and passed around a bowl of hard, yellowy nuggets. They were *aaruul*, another staple of every Mongolian table and a testament to the ingenuity of humankind. Who first discovered that you could make from milk a dried curd with the consistency of rock and the smell of vomit – *and then eat it?*

Hard and pungent, *aaruul* quickly became my least favourite Mongolian food, and the hardest to avoid, since Mongolians both keep it on their tables at home and carry handfuls to work or school as a snack food, and they are always handing it around. 'Very good for the teeth,' they would always say to me. I'd nibble politely, then stuff it in my pocket when no one was looking. Later, on my way home, I'd toss it to one of the city's myriad stray dogs. I was buying them off, one by one.

Someone in Mongolia had the enterprising idea that there was an export market for *aaruul*, because I'd see it in the market, packaged in cardboard and labelled in English under the appetising name of National Dried Curds.

Aaruul was only one among a huge variety of gamey dairy products the Mongolians wrung from their livestock. In summer, Mongolian herders subsist almost entirely on these 'white foods': curds, soft cheese, rancid butter, cottage cheese, sour cream. And *airag*, fermented mare's milk, Mongolia's national drink. More about that later.

Now Bolormaa was preparing the *buuz*, the centrepiece of the meal, the most beloved of all Mongolian foods. It is a simple steamed dumpling whose constituent ingredients – boiled mutton (again!), flour, onions and garlic – tell another classic Mongolian story.

Flour has been part of the Mongolian diet for centuries, but it has been an import item since Chinggis Khan first conquered the adjoining territory of the more sedentary, farming Chinese. In the twentieth century, Soviet planning carved out state farms on the steppe that made Mongolia self-sufficient in wheat, but with the collapse of the planned economy the farms have withered and the mills crumbled, and Mongolia must once again import its flour.

Onions and garlic add a dash of spice and are decidedly optional. They are practically the only remaining spice traces from the Mongols' imperialist quests across Asia and Europe, which introduced them to the cuisines of China, India and other countries. None of it seems to have stuck, though the more recent Russian influence has given city Mongolians a taste for potato salad, cold cuts, pickles, and Maggi sauce.

Bolormaa showed me how the simple ingredients of *buuz* are combined. She scooped a handful of minced, boiled mutton onto a circle of dough, and with a deft twist and pinch she turned it into a fat little ball with a crenellated edge. Soon she had several dozen of them lined up, ready to be steamed on the stove.

'It's easy,' she said. 'Here, try.'

Take my word for it. It isn't easy.

Soon the dumplings were steamed and presented on a large platter to the guests, who reached for them with a chorus of appreciative little grunts. I have seen weather-beaten Mongolian faces take on a rapturous expression with the first bite from the hot, sticky bundles: the chewy dough giving way to a rush of steam, a mouthful of mutton and a spurt of hot fat.

For many foreigners, the first taste of *buuz* has an equally visceral, but almost exactly opposite, effect.

Mongolians love their food and tuck in with gusto – an admirable trait, in my opinion. They eat prodigiously and are rewarded for their meat- and milk-based diet by being significantly taller and broader than their Asian neighbours. When they go abroad, they suffer withdrawal – just as I, in Mongolia, developed an unexpected longing for macaroni and cheese. One woman I know who went to study in the United States had to have tea bricks posted to her; the bag stuff they sold over there just didn't taste the same.

Another acquaintance, Miji, a driver for the United Nations, had been on a trip to England. His reaction was typical. 'It was all right,' he said, 'because they eat quite a bit of meat there. But the meat abroad just doesn't taste like *meat*.'

He had a point. Mongolian meat is 100 per cent free range, organic and chemical free. Herders do not feed their livestock but simply set them loose to graze, and the animals must often cover large distances in search of food. This has the effect of making the meat a tad tough. 'Mongolian cows,' a local agronomist once told me, 'are what we call 'sports animals.'"

Still – entrepreneurs take note – I've often thought there was a business opportunity in marketing pure Mongolian meat to Western consumers alarmed at our overprocessed and factory-farmed meat. I did hear of a project, involving a mobile slaughterhouse, to export Mongolian lamb to the United Kingdom, but thanks to the country's remoteness and lack of infrastructure nothing has been done on a large scale. Mongolians themselves do not eat lamb and believe there is something a bit indecent about slaughtering a sheep before it is grown.

Back in the *ger* and now stuffed to bursting with *buuz*, I asked Bolormaa what other dishes she might prepare for dinner. She reeled off variations on the mutton-and-carbohydrates theme: *khuushuur*, another snacking favourite, is a dumpling, much like *buuz*, only flattened, fried and often soggy with grease; *tsoimon* is fried mutton and noodles; a soup of boiled mutton with a few carrots and chipped potatoes in a greasy broth is also popular.

Although mutton is the staple flesh, goat is also eaten, and there are regional preferences. In the Gobi, camel meat is fairly common, and the Kazakhs in the west have a taste for horsemeat.

Before the long winter, Bolormaa explained, herding families will slaughter several sheep – by holding the animal down, cutting a neat slit in the chest, sticking in a hand, grabbing the heart until it stops; that way, the blood is not lost and can be used for cooking. They cut the meat into strips and dry it in the sun; the jerky will be cooked with rice or noodles for a winter supper. Summer brings barbecues and outdoor cookouts, festive occasions on which chunks of meat and rocks are placed in a steel drum and cooked over a fire; once the meat is cooked, the hot rocks are passed around – they are meant to have therapeutic properties – before the meat is ripped into, lustily, with the hands.

In summertime, too, the men hunt marmots, pudgy groundhog-like rodents that are cooked in an even more extravagant outdoor fashion: the carcass is stuffed with hot rocks, inserted through the anus, and a blowtorch is used to burn off the fur. The marmot's dense meat is considered something of a treat, though eating it is not without its risks – every year in Mongolia, several people die of bubonic plague transmitted via the rodents.

Still, the marmot barbecue is a rite of passage for foreigners in Mongolia, even if some get a bit confused about the details. A friend of mine, driving across the eastern steppe, encountered a party of Russians attempting, with drunken high spirits, to cook a marmot by blowtorching it up the butt.

Despite the limited range of the Mongolian diet, home-cooked Mongolian food is often prepared with love and offered with hospitality. On one occasion, I visited the *ger* of an elderly couple with an American friend. It was a typical *ger* visit, his first. As respected guests, we were seated near the back of the *ger* and offered bowls of tea and chunks of curd while we chatted with the husband. The wife rattled around on the other side of the stove and, after half an hour or so, presented us with a heaping, steaming platter of *buuz*. It was crowned with a thick slab of fat the size of a paperback. This was presented to my colleague as the senior (male) guest. He paled visibly but forced it down like a trooper. The old woman beamed; as we left, he was offered leftovers for the road and a place to stay the next time he was in Mongolia. I swear he had tears in his eyes.

Restaurants were another matter. When I arrived in Mongolia, Ulaanbaatar had no shortage of eating establishments, but most were spartan canteens – *guanz* in Mongolian – designed, in that Soviet way, as soulless worker-feeding stations. They served only mutton with rice/with noodles/in soup and tea, and ranged from passably clean places with just-about-edible food to grubby shacks with dim lighting designed to prevent you from seeing the hairs, gristly bits and mystery chunks in your dinner.

Foreigners reacted in one of two ways. The more affluent – consultants, 'development practitioners,' and the like – shuddered in horror and shipped in caviar and smoked salmon by mail order. Backpackers, Peace Corps volunteers, and others too poor to have delicacies shipped in developed a sort of culinary Stockholm syndrome. The fattier the mutton, the more rancid the *airag*, the better they liked it.

There were a few higher-end restaurants serving European or Turkish food. They promised salvation, but eating in them was often a heartbreaking experience. Soon after I arrived in Mongolia, I discovered a restaurant of irresistible symbolism. I'd wandered into a public building, a typical concrete slab, that had housed the Lenin Museum (now closed). The cavernous lobby was dominated by an enormous white bust of Vladimir Ilyich, backed by a blood-red mural proclaiming 'Workers of the World Unite!' in half a dozen languages. Down at ground level were tables and chairs and white tablecloths and plastic flowers in vases. It was, miraculously, a Turkish restaurant. A large sign proclaimed its name: Turkish Restaurant. (The science of marketing languished at a fairly rudimentary level in Mongolia.)

The juxtaposition of present and past was irresistible, and I sat down with a sense of occasion and excitement. A waitress, in uniform, brought me a menu. It listed *kofte* and *doner* and other mouth-watering treats. I was unused to such a selection; it took me some time to settle on my choice.

'*Doner*,' I said.

The waitress sucked a quick rush of air in through her teeth. '*Bakui*,' she said.

Ah, *bakui* – the first Mongolian word all foreigners learn. It's a simple negative – it means 'isn't' or 'aren't' – with an astonishingly flexible range of meanings, from 'The person you wish to speak to is not in the office at the moment' to (as on this occasion) 'The item you have requested is, regrettably, not available.'

I had already heard the word many times in restaurants, always spoken with the same sad certainty. But on this occasion I clung to hope. '*Kofte*, then,' I ventured.

'*Bakui*.'

'Kebab?'

It was no use; all the main courses were *bakui*. Then what, exactly, was available?

My waitress pointed to the other side of the menu. 'Soup,' she said.

The menu listed two soups, each with an authentically Turkish-sounding name. I was hungry. 'I'll have one of each, please.'

Half an hour later, my soups arrived. They were identical – clods of boiled mutton and potato in greasy broth.

But things were changing. First there was Café de France, a surprisingly authentic corner *boite* tucked away on a downtown street of shady trees and peeling stucco. The area had a passed-over Eastern European feel about it and was the nearest the scruffy Mongolian capital got to charm; I liked to think of it as Ulaanbaatar's Left Bank.

Café de France was run by a louche Corsican, and its sunny decor succeeded brilliantly; here you could drink pastis or real coffee and eat apricot tart and imagine yourself far away. It was full of homesick French people doing just that. The food was more hit-and-miss: passable but tough steak *frites*, soups that had the tang of the packet about them. And the service was erratic – five people ordering at once would often receive their meals one at a time, at 15-minute intervals. It didn't matter, though. Back in those hungry days, expats in Mongolia would forgive Café de France anything.

Café de France was run by foreigners and largely for

foreigners, as well as for nouveau riche Mongolians. But soon it had competition from Mongolian entrepreneurs.

Ulaanbaatar didn't have anything so grand as a university district, but it did have a sort of youth corner, a busy concrete plaza opposite both the Mongolian National University and the Technical University. It was always thronging with young people chatting in the sun, and had a greater than usual concentration of kiosks, ice-cream vendors and newspaper stands. One of the kiosks had long stood empty, and I scarcely noticed it as I hurried by shivering, but one day something pulled me up and made me look again. It sported a fresh coat of paint and a bright red and green sign: Pizza de la Casa.

The kiosk now also had a door. I pushed it open, scarcely daring to hope. Inside, it was just big enough to hold a bright blue bar and a row of stools; it was steamy and crowded. I elbowed my way up to the counter.

'What would you like?' asked a smiling young man, indicating a wall adorned with plastic-coated photos of more than a dozen varieties of pizza: Sicilian, Hawaiian, Mongolian (topped with chunks of mutton).

'Umm, a Sicilian please.'

'Coke with that?'

'Uh, sure.' I was in shock.

Five minutes later, I was biting into something hot and cheesy and unmistakably pizza. Many of my expat acquaintances had materialised, too, along with a gaggle of Mongolian students. All wore expressions of childlike delight.

The genius behind Pizza de la Casa was Eddie, who ran the operation with his brother-in-law, Bojo. A friendly and determined man in his early thirties, Eddie (his real name was Enkhi) had studied engineering in Germany with the help of a United Nations grant. While there, he'd got a job in an Italian restaurant, and it was in Germany, unlikely as it sounds, that he learned to make pizza. He also had a business idea, and when he returned to Mongolia it was with a pizza oven, which he had somehow squeezed into a corner of a disused kiosk, partitioning off a tiny kitchen.

Never let it be said that the United Nations has done nothing for Mongolia. Pizza de la Casa was a stroke of genius, catering both to homesick expats and to aspirational Mongolians. The pizzas were cheap enough even for foreign backpackers and volunteers, though still pricey for ordinary Mongolians, but Eddie also sold even cheaper sandwiches and burgers and did a great trade with the student crowd. The Mongolian pizza also proved to be a hit.

Pizza de la Casa flourished. Within months, in addition to the kiosk, Eddie had opened a sit-down restaurant complete with paintings on the walls, candles on the tables and a range of pasta dishes on the menu. Then, soon after, came a second, more upscale, restaurant, with three separate rooms, each lavishly decorated in the style of a different Italian region (sunny Sicily, watery Venice), as well as another pizza outlet on a busy shopping street in one of Ulaanbaatar's high-rise suburbs.

Eddie was a pioneer, and others soon emerged to try

to capture Mongolia's newfound taste for Italian nosh: not one but two Italian restaurants, just steps from one another, both with Italian chefs and a nice line in *antipasti*. A veritable Little Italy. Soon Ulaanbaatar's dining scene began to diversify with what seemed like dizzying speed. A French-African café run by an expatriate Cameroonian. The country's first-ever international chain restaurant: a brightly designed branch of a Singapore-based Indian franchise, which opened, bravely, in the depths of an Ulaanbaatar winter, the eyes of its efficient imported managers watering with the cold.

You couldn't always guarantee that the items on the menu would be available or that the restaurant would have heat or electricity. But it seemed like heaven.

Of course, these restaurants, though cheap by Western standards, were outrageously expensive to most Mongolians. They existed to serve a small, affluent, and desperate crowd of development workers, businesspeople and consultants, as well as a Mongolian elite that was tiny, but growing, and increasingly sophisticated. You didn't see many ordinary Mongolians in such places.

But I was always being surprised. Once I was with a Canadian friend, who worked for a UN project, and his colleague Davaasuren, a cheerful, efficient, highly educated and staunchly communist Russophile in her forties. We were batting around the idea of going somewhere to eat. Davaasuren immediately kicked into organiser mode; she was a great organiser, Davaasuren.

'I know a good restaurant,' she said, bundling us into our coats.

I was anticipating the Eastern European, potato salad-and-cutlet variety. But soon we were in a taxi bumping along the unpaved lanes of one of the city's *ger* suburbs. Davaasuren was peering closely at a succession of sagging wooden gates and ramshackle single-storey buildings.

I was puzzled. 'Are we going to a *guanz*?' I asked.

'No. A Chinese restaurant. Very good.'

'Chinese restaurant?' we screeched. It was the last kind of restaurant you expected to find in Mongolia. Mongolia and China have a long, tense history. Most Mongolians I'd met had nothing good to say about the Chinese, their culture, language or business practices. I certainly did not expect them to embrace Chinese food.

But Davaasuren was telling us a different story. This *ger* district – dusty and weather-beaten and indistinguishable from all the others – had once had a large Chinese community alongside Chinese restaurants and shops. We were driving through Ulaanbaatar's Chinatown.

'What happened?' I asked.

'When the Russians and the Chinese had their dispute, in the 1960s, the Chinese were expelled,' Davaasuren explained. Some had lived in Mongolia for decades. Their children had been born there.

Ulaanbaatar, I discovered, retains a small and extremely low-profile Chinese community. I met only a handful of Chinese: the staff of the embassy's visa section; the affable Mr Li from the Xinhua news agency, who spoke Mongolian well and would always greet me with, 'In one more year, I can go back to Beijing!' The city also had Chinese restaurants, which tended, literally, to be hidden.

Davaasuren never did find the restaurant of her memories that day, but later I managed to find another one: it was tucked away under the main traffic bridge out of town, beside a tyre yard and was identifiable only by a sign for Yanjing beer. It was the real thing too. Plain and teeming and thick with the scent of garlic. The tables were filled by Chinese couples and – wait a minute! – Mongolian families, digging in as enthusiastically as if they were eating *buuz*.

I'd discovered a secret. Mongolians do not live in a culinary vacuum. Many Mongolians like to eat Chinese food. They just don't like to admit it.

The greatest restaurant triumph of my time in Mongolia was Millie's, a café that transformed the lives of Ulaanbaatar's expatriate population. It wasn't officially called Millie's; it was called Buna Espresso. But it was run by a commanding American of Ethiopian origin named Millie, and everyone called it Millie's.

Millie's opened in the spring. Word had been going around for weeks that it was to be something special, a proper café serving genuine cappuccino and homemade cakes.

It was everything we'd hoped for. The redoubtable Millie – through a force of will I can scarcely comprehend – had refurbished a space with white walls and wooden furniture and funky art. She had flown in a stock of Ethiopian coffee from San Francisco and – even more impressively – kept it coming. She kept a shelf stocked with American magazines. And she had employed the services of Daniel, a member of Mongolia's single-digit Cuban community, as chef.

Millie's served frothy cappuccino and rich chocolate cake and real – real! – hamburgers. Daniel cooked up chicken tacos and *huevos rancheros*. It was a revelation. Within weeks, it became all but impossible to get a seat at lunchtime, so packed was Millie's with consultants and backpackers and (a few) smartly dressed Mongolians. Over lingering Sunday brunches, you'd run into everyone you knew in Ulaanbaatar.

It was just like any other city. And I probably wasn't the only one who thought, as I sipped contentedly at my cappuccino, that I was somehow cheating.

One day I was sitting with a table of assorted expats at lunchtime. As our generous helpings of food arrived – prompt and hot – Susan, a perky American who'd survived two years in the Peace Corps, let out the tiniest tut of annoyance. 'Oh, I hate it when Millie puts too much vinaigrette on the salad; it soaks into my quiche.'

There was a nanosecond of utter silence.

'I can't believe I just said that,' said Susan solemnly. 'Dorothy, we're not in Mongolia anymore.'

Chapter Thirteen

A Stiff Drink

Before I headed off to Mongolia, I sought out people who had been there before. I didn't find any, but I did know a clutch of committed Russophiles and Sovietologists who'd done hard time in Siberia. They'd reminisce, leafing through albums full of pictures of rows of people in tall fur hats against all-white landscapes; they'd pull their own tall fur hats from the backs of cupboard shelves and stroke them, wearing expressions of misty remembrance. Then their eyes would glaze over.

'My God,' they'd whisper. 'The vodka.'

Vodka, they warned me, lubricated all social gatherings in the Soviet world, from drop-in parties to weddings to state banquets; it cemented business deals, and it greased the wheels of government. It was the liquid fuel, harsh and combustible, that kept the system running. And Mongolia had had seven decades of Russian tuition in the art of vodka consumption.

The *Lonely Planet Mongolia* guide, first edition, was stern in its warning. It suggested all errands and commerce in Ulaanbaatar be accomplished before noon; after that, a large segment of the population would be staggering and aggressive or catatonic.

It wasn't that bad. My first afternoon reconnoitre of the city's main thoroughfare, Peace Avenue, did turn up several middle-aged women bearing hard, stoic looks and lurching, legless husbands. But most people looked passably sober.

Vodka – *arkhi* in Mongolian – was everywhere, though, cheap and plentiful, sold in stout clear bottles in hundreds of hole-in-the-wall bars, spartan corner shops, and creaking kiosks. Thick, glutinous, antiseptic liquid, sold under a bewildering array of brand names: Bolor *arkhi*, Chinggis Khan *arkhi*, Tsagaan *arkhi* and simply Arkhi *arkhi*. It was consumed in bars, on the street, at home, in the office – despite notices, like the one in my own workplace, threatening dismissal for anyone caught boozing at work.

Many men – I never saw a woman drunk – were unfamiliar with the notion of drinking in moderation. They started to drink and didn't stop until they were unconscious. But I had been to England; I was used to this.

There was no particular social stigma attached to public drunkenness, and many men shrugged off the consequences of their benders – the fistfights with friends, the raging hangovers, the tussles with police – with humour and grace.

One Monday morning, I asked a fellow reporter, a stout, jolly fellow, how he'd spent the weekend.

'In jail,' he said cheerfully. 'I went out with some friends, and it got a bit out of hand. The police came and hauled us all off to the Bayanzurkh drunk tank. They took our clothes away and gave us each a blanket to sleep in. It was crowded, but I was tired. In the morning, they lined us all up outside and hosed us off to wake us up. Then they gave us a lecture on drunkenness. I think I'll write an article about it.' He went off satisfied; his research was done.

The police spent much of their time dealing with alcohol-related problems. Ulaanbaatar had seven drunk tanks, to which police delivered 150 people a night – to sober them up, to stop them from fighting, or to prevent them from freezing to death. One senior police officer estimated that a quarter of crimes in the city were committed by people who were drunk, not counting drink-driving offences.

I tried to see the good side. Distilling was, after all, a domestic industry – one of the few the country had left. While production of most goods plummeted in the 1990s after the Russians withdrew their support, Mongolia's vodka output soared. The country had more than 200 distilleries, with a combined output of 12 litres per year for every man, woman and child in Mongolia. And that's not counting the hundreds of illegal businesses producing cheap, homemade – and occasionally lethal – hooch that sold for as little as 20 pence a litre.

The vodka really didn't taste that bad, I discovered, and was prone to lead to sentimental outbursts of song and arms-around-shoulders declarations of friendship. But it was a volatile addition to an unstable society.

Everyone in Mongolia has had an unpleasant experience with a drunk. Here's mine.

I came home from work one dusk. Two young men were lounging beside the broken and twisted remains of a bench that stood in front of my building. I pushed open the stiff and heavy aluminium door and stepped into the tiny, dark, urine-scented entranceway. The light, as ever, was broken, but I knew my way up to my third-floor flat blind. But the two men had followed me in. One tapped me on the shoulder. He was tall and lean and very drunk. The vapour seemed to rise off his clothes in wavy lines, like in a cartoon. He was at least six inches taller than I was, and he stood between me and the door. His friend stood between me and the stairs. He said something in Mongolian, in a slurred bark. I caught the word *money*.

'*Bakhui*,' I said, giving a little apologetic shrug.

A bolt of frustration shot across his clouded eyes. He repeated his demand, louder, and gave me a shove.

'No, really,' I said, digging in my heels. '*Bakhui*. Sorry.' I shot a look at his friend: back me up on this one. He looked away and swayed a little.

It occurred to me that I was being mugged and that my Mongolian really wasn't up to the situation. 'Look,' I said, pointing at him, at his friend, and at myself. '*Naiz*.' Friends.

He gave a snort of derision, and then he reached out and knocked my glasses to the ground with the back of his hand. He gripped my arm above the elbow, leaned forward, and gave me a blast of his steamy vodka breath. He spoke more slowly, more menacingly, a long and angry tirade in which the word *American* figured prominently.

'You shouldn't have knocked off my glasses,' I replied in English, through set teeth, the indignant memory of every schoolyard bully I'd ever encountered coursing through my veins. *'You don't do that.* And I'm not American.'

'I am a bodybuilding master,' he said ominously.

I didn't answer. We stared at each other through the gloom, neither willing to back down. I think we stood like that for ten minutes. Finally the other man couldn't take it anymore. He pried his friend's fingers from my arm and propelled him gently toward the door. On the threshold, he turned. 'Sorry,' he said.

There was a lot of talk about drink, from the newspapers, which ran articles with headlines such as 'MONGOLIA IS DROWNING IN A SEA OF VODKA' (a classic that I wrote myself), to the president, who launched a personal crusade against the demon drink. Everyone wanted to see it as a metaphor – for colonialism or communism, for capitalism or economic catastrophe. It was the fault of the Russians for teaching Mongolians to drink vodka, or the Chinese for supplying the even more lethal cheap white spirit, or the Americans for polluting the youth with Schwarzenegger and MTV. Everyone wanted someone to blame.

I didn't know. So I asked an eminent Mongolist – one of a small but hardy breed. Dr Judith Nordby of Leeds University said it was rubbish.

'Neither the Russians nor the Chinese taught Mongolians to drink,' she informed me. 'They didn't need to – the Mongolians had a taste for alcohol dating back to the empire period, at least.

'Chinggis Khan's son and successor, Ogodei, basically drank himself to death. His brother was so worried about him that he asked him to drink fewer goblets of wine. Ogodei promptly halved the number of goblets – and doubled their size.'

Western visitors to the Mongol court noticed the khans' hearty appetite for food and drink. The pattern continued right up to the 1921 revolution. Mongolia's last theocratic ruler, the eighth Bogd Khan, was infamous for going on benders that lasted several days.

Trade during the Mongol Empire brought brandy and wine, as well as tea, to the Mongols, but imported booze remained a drink for the elite. It took Communism and membership in the socialist countries' trading bloc, COMECON, to bring commercially produced bottled booze to the masses.

'The aristocrats of the COMECON period campaigned against drunkenness from time to time,' Dr Nordby told me. 'But the socialist elite drank as much as anyone. There was a lot of lip service but rather less commitment.'

Vodka was only one of the liquid threats I'd been warned about. 'Mongolia, eh?' said the avuncular doctor in the Toronto travel clinic, stabbing home my hepatitis jab. 'Will you live in a yak?'

'Yurt,' I said.

'Oh, that's right. Well, anyway, you have to be careful of brucellosis and giardia – that second one is a very common parasite. Don't eat any dairy products.'

This proved to be the most useless piece of travel advice I'd ever received. Mongolians live off the fat of their herds – as well as their meat, bones, assorted innards and milk. In cities the traditional diet is supplemented by prepared and packaged food, but in the countryside livestock supply families with almost everything they need to survive. Meat and milk reign supreme.

And if you think you can't make booze from livestock, well, you're wrong. The king of all Mongolian beverages is *airag* – fermented mare's milk. It's fizzy and sharp and the strength of light beer, and Mongolians cannot get enough of the stuff. It's essentially a summer drink, and in summer in town you can buy it from plastic drums outside the markets. In the country, you make it at home. The milk is fermented in a big hide sack – like a giant wineskin – with a churning pole sticking out of the neck, which sits in a corner of the *ger*. Every so often, one of the family will go over and give it a stir.

The first time I visited a *ger*, the family was renowned in the area for the quality of their *airag*, and the woman of the house proudly handed me a Chinese soup bowl full of the latest vintage. I looked at it. It resembled yellowish milk, edged with a ring of tiny bubbles; a couple of short black hairs drifted on the surface. I stared at the bowl for a long moment, calculating how much I could get down in one gulp, then tossed it back.

Imagine sharp, watery yogurt. Imagine liquid goat cheese. It rushed past my gag reflex, plummeted to my stomach, and settled down to continue its churning fermentation. 'Delicious,' I said queasily.

'In summertime, we herders eat nothing but *airag*, and we are never hungry,' the man of the house told me proudly. It was true. I later read that a typical rural family of five drinks at least 200 litres of *airag* a week in the summer.

'No, I can see why not,' I said, clutching my stomach, where the lively beverage was coursing in a series of whirls and rapids. If you drank *airag* all day, you'd also be slightly drunk. Mongolia in summertime is a nation of pleasantly buzzed people on horseback. No wonder the herders look contented.

Our host was preparing to show us the surrounding countryside. He lugged a 40-litre petrol jug full of *airag* into the back of the jeep. By the end of the day, it was empty.

Airag is ubiquitous. One day I was driving in the countryside, in a remote area of northern Mongolia, huddled in the back of a 40-year-old Russian jeep as it negotiated a particularly wretched, rutted track over a series of mountain passes – the jeep straining to the top, then juddering to the bottom as the driver turned off the engine to save fuel. We'd been proceeding like this, making maybe 12 miles an hour, for almost five hours. Around the jeep nothing but blue sky, green grass, brown rock, stands of larch and the cloud of dust that surrounded and followed us. Then, at the top of one pass, sat two small girls behind a folding table next to a big blue jug.

'It's a lemonade stand!' I cried, delirious with happiness.

We stopped alongside, and the driver passed a 100-tugrug note to one of the girls. She opened the jug and ladled some of the contents into a chipped ceramic bowl. It was *airag*. He gulped it down with one fluid motion, wiped his mouth with the back of his hand, and handed back the empty bowl. The girl held it out in my direction, motioned toward the jug. For once, I decided to heed the doctor's warning. 'No thanks,' I said.

The worst thing about the Mongolian countryside, many foreigners agreed, was that you couldn't get a cold beer to save your life. I mean, here was a country that looked for all the world like Montana – the rugged openness, the don't-fence-me-in cowboy spirit, the camping and barbecues – but never a Bud to cap off the day. The best you could hope for were warm tins of weak Chinese lager or cloudy bottles of flat Russian-style *pivo*.

No wonder, then, that Mongolians had never really developed a taste for beer. But that was changing. With the new waves of foreigners, the Germans and the Brits, a new liquid tide was sweeping Ulaanbaatar.

Dave, Rob, and I stumbled upon the revolution during a summer-evening stroll through the town. As we walked across Sukhbaatar Square and down Chinggis Avenue toward the Bayangol Hotel, we passed a round, *ger*-shaped building just off the main square. A former children's cafeteria, it now bore a bright red and yellow sign: Khan Brau.

'That's a bar now,' said Rob. 'Let's check it out.'

We pushed our way in past a polite bouncer – and into a teeming Bavarian *brauhaus*. The chunky wooden tables were packed out by a mixed crowd of sozzled expats and young Mongolians – boisterous foursomes of Mongolian women, chatting and laughing; less boisterous young women cozying up to bleary-eyed German businessmen; stylish students in cashmere sweaters and leather jackets, shyly eyeing one another.

On a tiny stage, a band (a live band!) was launching into a raucous, if inexact, rendition of 'Lady Madonna.' Red-aproned waitresses were hauling hearty platters of schnitzel and roast pork, ice-cream sundaes and frothy steins of made-in-Mongolia pilsener. There was not a bottle of vodka in sight.

'Wow,' said Rob.

We looked in vain for a place to sit.

'Please join us,' said a young woman whose high Mongolian cheekbones were alarmingly offset by a rainbow-striped sweater and cheap peroxide.

We sat.

'My name's Cathy,' she said, in English. 'I'm from California.'

Rob raised his eyebrows, and Cathy explained, sort of, that her husband was a businessman in America. She did not specify what kind of business he did. Cathy was at the Khan Brau with a female friend and a sheepish-looking middle-aged man. He was not her husband, though he may well have been some woman's husband.

Cathy began asking Dave and Rob about themselves, leaning close, ignoring me. I took the hint and slunk off to watch the band.

'Sorry,' I said, bumping into a teenager.

'That's OK,' she said in perfect American English.

'How long did you spend in the States?' I asked.

'Oh, I've never been there.'

It turned out she and her friends attended a local college run by the University of Colorado. They were all big fans of the Khan Brau.

'I come here a lot – whenever my Mom lets me,' said the first student, who said her name was Khulan and claimed to be 20. 'I like to have a beer and listen to rock and roll. Beer drinking is becoming more popular. It's to do with more foreign influences and ideas coming into the country.'

I glanced at a menu card. A pint of beer cost almost one pound fifty.

'But isn't it awfully expensive?' I asked.

'Yes, but that's a good thing,' said Khulan. 'It means there aren't as many fights.'

'Beer's good, because you don't get as drunk as you do with vodka,' agreed her friend. 'And I think a certain amount of beer is good for your body.'

Welcome to Mongolia, I thought. The only country in the world where beer is considered a health food.

'The band's good,' I said, motioning toward the stage, where a chunky lead singer was essaying Smokie's 'Living Next Door to Alice' for a rapturous crowd. (What *was* it with that song?) 'What're they called?'

'Shar Airag.'

I smiled. The name meant Yellow Airag – the Mongolian word for beer. Clearly this band was at the centre of the whole beer-drinking scene. When they finished their set and sidled over to the bar for a drink, I approached the singer and introduced myself.

'How do you do,' he said in English. He was squat

and baby-faced. 'I am Gankhuu, deputy director of Khan Brau.'

'This is your business? And you play in the band?'

'I am also the president of the Mongolian Beer Association,' he said. 'You could say that beer is my life.'

Leaning on the bar, he told me about his business. 'In 1996, I was a student in the Czech Republic, and a friend of mine, who is now Khan Brau's general director, was studying in Germany. He suggested we could make a new product for Mongolia, because at the time there was only one brewery, the state-owned brewery, and its technology was very old. My friend had a German friend who'd made his money in computers, and he agreed to become our investor.

'We imported the beer-making equipment – all new technology – and the malt and hops from Germany and hired a German *braumeister*, and we opened in October of 1996. We made the first pilsener ever brewed in Mongolia.'

The way Gankhuu told the story, that was just the beginning of a lager revolution. Khan Brau opened the flagship bar, then two more, including a faux-Irish pub called the Boar's Tooth, complete with dark wood interior and Guinness posters. They'd successfully campaigned for the repeal of a law banning outdoor drinking and opened this wintry country's first beer garden. They'd got their draft beer into 36 bars and had begun selling bottled beer in shops. They'd introduced live bar bands – 'All the nightclub acts mime to tapes,' said Gankhuu dismissively – and encouraged young talent. And they had pioneered Western-style marketing savvy – slick billboards sporting images of home-grown rock stars, contests, a beer-bottle mascot roaming Sukhbaatar Square.

'It sounds like more than a drink,' I suggested. 'It sounds like a lifestyle revolution.'

'We have made a small revolution in Mongolia,' Gankhuu agreed. 'When we started, people were drinking hard liquor almost exclusively. The beer brewed by APU, the state company, was not very popular. Now young people like to drink beer.

'Our beer isn't cheap, because everything but the water is imported from Germany. But it's not for everyone. If we lower the price, we lose our elite customers. They don't mind paying 1,900 tugrug for a beer if they can sit in a nice place listening to live music. We could sell a beer for 500 tugrug, but then what kind of people would come? There would be fights and trouble.'

This elite cachet, he explained, was crucial to beer's appeal. His greatest fear was that the authorities would lump beer in with vodka as a social evil and subject it to tirades and sin taxes.

'Beer is better than vodka. There aren't so many social problems like crime and alcoholism with beer. Beer comes with a good atmosphere. You can have two or three beers and go home. Beer should not be put on the list with hard liquor. Beer should be like bread.'

'Cheers to that,' I said.

Chapter Fourteen

The Three Manly Sports

The air in the wrestling stadium was moist and ripe, as fetid as a small-town hockey arena; the stands were packed with musky, unwashed, midwinter bodies. In the centre of the round building lurched several pairs of large, sweaty men clad in embroidered silk bikini briefs, tiny, open-fronted, cutoff jackets, and stout leather boots with upturned toes. A rivulet of water trickled down through a crack in the newly-built roof.

One pair of wrestlers staggered to the edge of the circle, just a yard from where we were sitting, followed by a hovering, hawk-eyed referee. With a sudden jerk, the bigger man sent his opponent sprawling onto the carpet. A fine mist of sweat lashed off his body and rained down on the first few rows of the audience.

'That,' said Dave, 'is disgusting.'

The winning wrestler turned away from his felled opponent with a look of cool indifference, retrieved his tall, spiky-topped velvet hat from a second who stood at the ringside, set it neatly on his head, spread his arms, stood on one leg, and executed a slow-motion bird dance; as the loser ducked under his arm, the winner turned to acknowledge the applause of the crowd. An official offered him a bowl of hard biscuits and curds; he scooped up a handful and flung it into the stands. I flinched. A small, chubby fist snatched a biscuit from the air in front of my face. Its owner's plump cheeks flushed with pleasure and triumph.

'That's fucking disgusting as well,' hissed Dave.

Ritual served, the tournament resumed. The losers retired, and the winners paired off, so the field was whittled down, until only two wrestlers remained in the ring. And then only one was standing, a glistening behemoth basking in the adoration of his fans.

Mongolians love to watch wrestling, and they love to wrestle. Their national sport mixes long history, rich traditions and admirably simple rules. Mongolian wrestling works like this (stop me if I get too technical): two opponents meet, grab and grapple until one forces the other to touch the ground with a knee or an elbow; there are no weight categories, age restrictions or time limits. Bouts may last seconds or hours. Wrestlers may rely on speed and agility or on strength – the best rely on both. Almost the only absolute is that the competitors must be male: the open-fronted jackets were devised, according to legend, after a woman entered, and won, a tournament. Male pride could not have that happen again.

Mongolians have wrestled for thousands of years. Wrestling is the first among equals of the 'three manly sports' – the others are horse racing and archery – whose origins are tied up with warfare. Wrestling tournaments have their own distinctive rituals, such as the eagle dance performed by the victors and the foodstuffs bestowed on the winner and showered by him upon the crowd.

Sweaty men in slippery, intimate combat was not my idea of fun, but I was determined to come to grips with the three manly sports. The time to do it, I thought, was Naadam, Mongolia's three-day summer holiday. The festival, which centres on national competitions in the three sports, is ancient. Under Communism, it had been given a socialist gloss with the addition of military parades and anticapitalist slogans. The tank columns had now been done away with, to my regret, but an atmosphere of pomp and sombre celebration remained: there were presidential speeches and military bands and a solemn procession bearing the Great White Emblem of the Mongolian nation – a tall staff crowned with a ring of nine white horses' tails – from Government House to the national stadium.

Eggi, a friendly pop music-obsessed chatterbox who worked as a receptionist for the United Nations, had volunteered to guide Dave and me through the intricacies of the Mongolian national holiday.

In return, he had some intricacies of his own he wanted us to explain. 'Can you explain to me these lyrics from *Breakfast in America*?' he asked as we walked across the park toward the rickety open-air stadium.

'Why is wrestling so popular?' I asked him, trying to divert the conversation away from Supertramp.

He thought for a moment. 'Mongolians are very independent. In wrestling, *bokh*, everyone is equal – fat, thin, short, tall. There are no divisions. You must rely only on your own wits. And the bigger man does not always win. Mongolians value strength but also speed and intelligence.'

'That's not true!' interjected Dave. 'I've watched. The big guy always wins.'

'You are bigger than me,' Eggi pointed out. 'And I'm not a very good wrestler. But I could beat you.'

'Hey!' said Dave.

Eggi stopped and handed me his baseball cap. He assumed the stance: hands raised, knees bent, torso inclined slightly forward. Warily, Dave bent to meet him and lunged. A moment later, he was on the ground.

'You see?' said Eggi, replacing his cap and giving his arms a perfunctory flap. 'And I'm a bad wrestler. But don't feel too bad. It's in our blood.'

We got to our seats just as the match was starting. Pairs of wrestlers were scattered across the grass, each with its own referee in crisp *del*. The stadium held 15,000 people, and it was full.

'At least we're away from the spray this time,' Dave muttered.

An ululating melody on a horse-head fiddle came through the tinny speakers, giving the event the appearance of a particularly clumsy square dance.

'The Naadam tournament features the 512 best wrestlers from across the country,' explained Eggi. 'There are nine rounds in all, with the losers from each round eliminated until only one champion remains. He becomes very famous and is given the title of Lion. There are other titles as well. A wrestler who wins five rounds in a row is called a Falcon; one who wins seven rounds is an Elephant. A two-time Naadam champion is called Giant, and a four-time champion – that's rare – is Invincible.

'You see that wrestler, the big one? That's Bat-Erdene, the greatest living wrestler. He has won ten Naadams;

his title is' – Eggi searched his brain for a moment – 'Renowned Across Mongolia, Greatest of the Great, Invincible Titan.'

'I've seen him before!' said Dave. 'He goes to my gym. He wears a police uniform.'

'That's his day job,' said Eggi.

In the ring, the field of 512 was being winnowed. Some bouts were over in seconds; others dragged on for many minutes, the straining, immobile pairs occasionally breaking apart on the command of the referee, only to clasp again.

'A few years ago,' said Eggi, 'when Bat-Erdene won, of course, the final went on for six hours. Most people went home before the end.'

I was beginning to feel that way myself. This tournament would last all day and all the next day as well. 'Shall we go and check out one of the other manly sports?' I suggested. 'Maybe the archery?'

Eggi sucked in a quick rush of air and took a quick, furtive look around. 'Archery is quite boring,' he confessed in a whisper. 'Let's go and see the horse races.'

We elbowed our way out of the stadium and down to the main road, where we managed to flag down a van to take us to the racing site. The horse races were held on a stretch of riverside plain west of town, near the airport. The race ground had the air of a carnival: a dusty, temporary city made of jeeps and bright blue tents pitched by competitors and spectators who'd travelled in from the countryside. And hundreds of horses, most ridden by children in colourful paper crowns and bright jerseys with numbers on the front.

'Are they going to a party?' I asked.

'They're the jockeys,' said Eggi. 'Mongolian race jockeys are always children, anywhere from four to sixteen years old.'

'Isn't that kind of dangerous?' I asked, alarmed.

'Oh, no. Mongolian countryside children learn to ride before they can walk. And, anyway, many of them have their feet tied to the stirrups so they don't fall off.'

'Where's the racetrack?' asked Dave.

Eggi made a sweeping motion with one hand. 'The racers start from here – that big blue tent is the grandstand, where the judges sit in the shade – and ride across the steppe. The courses are anywhere from ten to twenty miles long, depending on the ages of the horses. There are separate races for horses of different ages, but there are still as many as six hundred horses in each race.'

'Holy shit,' said Dave.

Suddenly there was a collective shout, a mass rustle of movement. The crowd surged toward the finish line, those on foot squeezing between the sleek flanks of the horses.

The front-runners appeared over the horizon, galloping hard, the tiny jockeys flailing one flank, then the other, with a short leather whip on a wooden handle. The first few horses charged into the funnel of spectators, shot past me so close I could feel their sweat – this seemed to be something of a theme in Mongolian sports – and crossed the finish line. They were followed close behind by the surging mass of the competitors, a rumbling cavalry that sent spectators skittering out of the way. Then a few stragglers, the tearful jockeys flailing at their truculent mounts.

We squeezed ourselves out of the seething mass of horse and human flesh and stood back to take in the scene. The little jockeys, no matter where they'd placed, were now the centre of their proud families' attention. They stood beside their horses, recounting the race. The winner and five runners-up, sitting straight and sombre with pride, remained mounted and executed a victory lap. They paused in front of the grandstand and were presented with a bowl by one of the judges.

'*Airag*,' said Eggi. Each child drank deeply, then sprinkled some *airag* on the rump of their horse as a herald sang the praises of each steed. Then, stiff and silent with the solemnity of the occasion, they received their medals.

'That's a nice ceremony,' said Dave.

'Wait,' said Eggi. 'There's one more prize.'

One more horse walked slowly up to the grandstand. Its rider's cheeks were red and streaked with tears. The crowd called out good-naturedly, and the herald recited a solemn ode.

'That's the horse that came in last,' said Eggi. 'They are wishing him success in the future.'

'Really?' I said. 'That's lovely.'

'I'm thirsty,' said Eggi. 'Let's go and have a beer.'

Mongolia's national sports have never really caught on outside the country – except in Chinese Inner Mongolia, where they survive in slightly different forms. So Mongolian athletes, eager to test themselves on the international stage, have had to adapt. Unsurprisingly they've had the most success in the internationally sanctioned forms of wrestling, winning several Olympic medals in free-style wrestling and judo and a number of titles in sambo, a sort of Soviet martial art, developed by the Russian armed forces and popular in the former Eastern-bloc countries.

A nation of hunters, they've also made their mark in shooting. Monkhbayar, an Olympic medal-winning markswoman, is a calendar star waiting to happen – she's young, svelte, has shimmering dark hair and carries a gun.

I reckoned, too, that a country with more than six months of winter would be a natural at winter sports. So when athletes from more than 70 countries marched into Nagano stadium for the opening ceremony of the 1998 Winter Olympics, I was hunched in front of my TV, awaiting the entrance of the Mongolian squad. Out they marched, tucked away in the middle of the alphabetical procession – two speed skaters and a cross-country skier, resplendent in ankle-length white fur coats, marching behind the blue, red and gold flag.

I felt a little flutter of pride. I imagined myself marching beside them, carrying with me the hopes of a nation. I imagined that, like most of the athletes marching into the stadium that day, the trio of Mongolians cherished the hope of going home with an Olympic medal. As it turned out, I imagined wrongly.

It was Otgoo, a colleague of mine from the sports

newspaper *Five Rings*, who burst my bubble. Otgoo was also a member of the Mongolian National Olympic Committee. 'When I check for our athletes' results,' he told me cheerfully, 'I start looking from the bottom.'

But surely, I protested, Mongolians are naturals at winter sports.

'Oh, yes, we have a good tradition of winter sports, from ancient times,' said Otgoo. 'Some Japanese researchers came to Mongolia, and they believe that skiing in Asia originated among Mongolian herders. The Tsataan people who live in Hovsgol *aimag*, the reindeer herders, used antlers to make skis. Skiing is very popular across a large area of central Mongolia.

'We've even held the Asian speed-skating championships in Ulaanbaatar,' he said with pride.

'So what's the problem?'

'In winter sports, we can compete at the Asian level, no problem,' he said. 'But not at the world level. In the West, athletes have the chance to train year-round. In Mongolia, it is very dependent on the season. We don't have modern facilities. In highly developed sports countries, they use indoor skating rinks. We only have open-air rinks.'

I took his point. I'd skated on one of Ulaanbaatar's handful of outdoor rinks – a drained pond in the park, more rock than ice – and I'd seen the country's one and only downhill ski run. It skittered down the hillside in a valley south of town, a short, uneven path, half snow and half dirt. The excruciatingly slow T-bar lift looked like something a mechanically inclined ten-year-old had rigged up from a lawn mower engine and a clothesline. Winter in Mongolia was long, but not long enough.

'It's a matter of the level of the country's economic development,' said Otgoo. 'But our desire to develop these sports and the talent of the Mongolian people – those remain.'

I saw these qualities in action some days later, when a Mongolian hockey team played a friendly tournament against a squad of Canadian, American and European expats who'd travelled up from Beijing. The Ulaanbaatar Cup, as it was grandly titled, was played in -25 °C temperatures at the city's best outdoor rink. Nestled amid blue blocks of flats in a hillside suburb called Brezhnev Heights, it boasted a commanding view of the city and surrounding mountains – but no stands, no penalty box, not even a bench. Before the game, the ice was cleared with a Mongolian ice-cleaning machine – a small boy dragging a wet blanket on a pole. Then a referee skated out, shooed a stray dog off the ice, and blew the whistle.

The play was choppy. The visitors, winded by the shattering cold and the shattered ice, were outmanoeuvred by a surprisingly disciplined team of burly Mongolians supplemented by several agile Russians who worked at one of the mines, and the home side triumphed by two games to one. Between shifts, the visiting players scurried to their waiting van and sat clutching their knees and shivering. When at last it was over and the losers limped off the ice – two to receive treatment for frost-bitten toes – I approached, in reporter mode, in search of the colourful quote I thought was de rigueur for a sports story.

'So,' I said to one of the wounded Canucks, 'what do you think is needed to improve hockey in Mongolia?'

'A bench,' he snapped.

The next week, I eagerly opened my copy of *Five Rings* to see how Mongolia's Olympians had done. The skaters had placed 28th and 29th in a field of 30. The skier had come 90th out of 98.

'He beat the skier from Kenya, though,' said Otgoo cheerfully. Then his broad, cheerful face clouded. 'The government has taken a decision to change the way athletes are funded. They've increased the prize money for athletes who achieve good results at continental championships, international championships and the Olympic Games. An athlete who wins an Olympic gold medal will receive close to US$100,000. But they've disbanded the national teams, and there's no financial support to organise national championships or for pre-Olympic training. Mongolia is not like Canada or the United States – in those countries, sports clubs are very rich, and governments have good policies toward businesses that donate to sports: tax breaks and that sort of thing. In Mongolia, no company is interested in donating money to sports, because it's not a priority. The economic situation is not good enough.

'Our athletes will look at the prize money, and they will try their best. That's very good. But cutting the expenses for training . . . it will have a bad influence on the survival of athletes. In Mongolia now, there are no more than twenty world-class athletes who can bring home medals from international games, and we have to keep these people.'

Chapter Fifteen

The Space Invaders

For a brief shining moment in the autumn of 1998, dusty old Mongolia sat on the high-tech cutting edge, on the gleaming cusp between science and science fiction.

It was an exciting and unsettling time, for me at least. One day in November, a jet skidded down the bumpy, frosty runway at Buyant-Ukhaa airport and disgorged a gaggle of Canadian and American astronomers, carrying some very expensive camera equipment, and a knot of officers from the United States Air Force. They were led by Colonel Peter Worden, the US Air Force Deputy for Battle Space Dominance. I'm not kidding. That's what it said on his business card, and we weren't going to question him, well trained and well mannered though he was. A bluff, close-cropped fellow, he wore a neatly pressed skin of congeniality over an iron core.

The Mongolian press corps sat, hushed and fidgeting, as the colonel briefed us on what had brought this high-flying team to the steppe.

Meteors.

In a few days' time, he explained, the earth was due to run smack into the Leonid stream, a ring of rock and metal particles racing around the sun in the wake of the Tempel-Tuttel comet. This in itself was not unusual; it happens every November, treating the earth to a display of the Leonid meteor shower. But once every three decades or so, the hail of meteors is particularly intense. And this, the scientists predicted, was going to be one of those years. On the last such occasion, in 1966, 100,000 meteors an hour could be seen at the shower's peak. This year's show could be even bigger, a once-in-a-lifetime event. It would look, said one of the astronomers, 'like the sky is falling in.'

Mongolia, with its ink-black skies and dry, clear weather, was a prime viewing spot. That explained why the civilian astronomers had come to set up their telescopes and cameras at the half-empty Soviet-era observatory in Ulaanbaatar's eastern hills. But it did not account for the barrel-chested colonel with the silver brush cut and his Pentagon throng.

The world had changed a great deal since 1966, he explained. Had we ever given a thought to the number of satellites currently in orbit around the earth? Silence all around. Obviously not. There were more than 600 of them; the US government alone had 100, serving both military and civilian purposes. Very important, very expensive bits of tin.

A few years ago, someone clever had pointed out that, if any one of the hundreds of millions of particles of space dust that made up the Leonid shower – travelling at a speed of 44 miles per second – hit a satellite, the result would be catastrophic. It would be, as one of the scientists helpfully put it, 'like a hot knife slicing through butter.'

'There are two forms of threat we're worried about,' explained Battle Space man. 'The first is if one of these meteorites – which is about the size of a grain of sand – hits a satellite. It'll have the force of a speeding bullet. And smaller pieces of material could create electrical faults and burn out the computer.' Mobile phones, global positioning systems and spy satellites could be knocked out – all sorts of minor and major disruptions the government and industry were keen to avoid. I thought I sensed just a hint of anticipation in the colonel's voice.

No one knew the odds of a satellite being knocked out – perhaps no more than 100 to one. But during the previous big meteor shower, the Perseid shower of 1993, a £500-million satellite belonging to the European Space Agency suffered 'catastrophic failure' after being hit by a meteoroid.

To protect the satellites, the boffins had hatched a plan: the astronomers at the observatory in Ulaanbaatar would track the meteor shower and relay real-time data (a 'flux profile' of the shower apparently) to a Canadian university laboratory, on to the US Air Force 55th Space Weather Squadron in Colorado Springs, Colorado, and thence to those private satellite operators who had paid for the service.

'The satellite operations centre will position the satellites for minimum damage,' explained Colonel Worden. 'We can't prevent the meteors from coming' – and I thought I detected a touch of regret – 'but we can do things to the satellites to lessen their vulnerability. We can turn them in space so they have less surface to be hit. In some cases, we can turn off the power so it's less likely there's an electrical short – though of course that makes them unavailable for use.'

There was definitely a strand of excitement shimmering beneath the colonel's stern exterior at all this talk of catastrophe in space. He later disclosed that he had been the head of technology in Reagan's Star Wars programme. Things couldn't have been the same for him since the United States turned away from planning battles in space and started fighting wars on the ground.

Now he was in Mongolia, wrapping up the press conference. 'This has never been attempted before,' he intoned. 'This is the first time all the satellites in space have been confronted with a threat of this type. That makes this a unique concern but also an opportunity to practise for other threats, whether natural or man-made. Like a hostile action in space.'

I just needed to check something. I raised my hand. 'You mean from earth, right?'

'From earth,' barked the colonel.

Colonel Worden informed us that a limited number of journalists would be allowed to spend Meteor Night (or M-Night, as I began to think of it) at the observatory. We would have to remain there from sunset till daybreak, because car headlights would disturb the scientists' observations. Cameras would not be allowed. We were very lucky to witness this historic event. We must not misbehave.

I was first in line to request my place. In fact, looking around, I was just about the only one in line. The press conference concluded, the Mongolian journalists drifted away in eddies of handshakes and quiet greetings, seemingly unmoved by this earth-shaking event.

On M-Night, we were driven bumpily by jeep out to

the observatory, which nestled idyllically on a hillside, surrounded by rocks and a puffy duvet of snow. A rare overcast day had given way to a crystal-clear night. The compound contained a huddle of buildings constructed in that cheap classical style favoured by the Soviets for scientific institutions. Rather grand from a distance, up close they surrendered to drab paint and dank mould and the scent of boiled mutton.

Colonel Worden showed the small band of visitors to a high-ceilinged hall set up as a reception room: rickety tables laid out with biscuits and warm fizzy drink, hard chairs. The shower was expected to peak at 2 a.m., he told us and clicked off, leaving us in the care of a junior officer, Lieutenant Tiffany Montague ('Like Shakespeare!' she commanded). She kept watch over the room like a friendly but eternally vigilant host.

It was 10 p.m., so I had plenty of time to sniff around the observatory compound. One wing, a semiderelict guest house, had been taken over by the scientists and their delicate equipment. It was off-limits.

On the hill behind the buildings, a group of figures in neon ski suits lay immobile in the snow, patently not making snow angels. Someone told me they were a band of keen and well-insulated German amateur astronomers, counting meteors.

The rest of the place was dark and had a damp, abandoned air – until I pushed open a door and found a bright and fully functional bar. It was warm and cozy, it offered hot mutton dumplings and tepid tinned beer, and it was packed. I elbowed my way in and found a mix of Mongolian observatory workers and drivers and a gang of students from the International School of Ulaanbaatar, up on an educational sleepover, who had taken over the pool table.

I also found a pair of journalists from Canada's two national newspapers, flown in by their papers to witness the auspicious event. We passed the time as journalists do.

By midnight, we'd assembled a keen but slightly bleary-eyed party: the US ambassador and his entourage; the troika of Canadian journalists; a smattering of bored and dozing Mongolian reporters; an energetic correspondent from *Sky and Telescope* magazine. Colonel Worden popped in every hour or so for a pep talk.

Last night's warm-up shower, he told us, had been fantastic. Orange fireballs streaking across the sky. It had looked, said the colonel, 'like God's own fireworks. It was,' he confessed, 'a little bit unexpected.'

Something in his voice made me sit up. I did not like the sound of that 'unexpected.' It was the middle of the night, on the side of the mountain, and it was 25 °C below. I did not want 'unexpected.' I wanted 'God's own fireworks.'

The colonel was still talking. The scientists were still predicting a peak of between 1,000 and 10,000 meteors per hour. (Not quite 100,000, but I'd settle for it.) 'There's a big question, actually, about whether this year or the next year is the big one. Predicting meteors is a bit like weather forecasting. Sometimes they're right, and sometimes they're wrong.'

I started to get that sinking feeling. The Beijing

correspondent for 'Canada's National Newspaper' decided to go on the record. 'This assignment,' he hissed, 'was not my idea.'

One of the dayglo Germans staggered in from the cold in search of a toilet. I asked how the meteor watch was going. He mumbled something incomprehensible through his hood.

At 1 a.m. – one hour to go – the colonel predicted a 'modest storm' of 1,000 meteors per hour, one every three seconds or so.

At the announced hour, we bundled up and trooped outside and stood shivering and craning our necks in the dark. A handful of shooting stars streaked across the sky. No fireballs. The sky was clearly not falling in. Our feet went numb. We went inside.

'Of course,' the colonel was saying, 'it's very difficult to predict exactly when the storm will peak.'

Somebody (it might have been me) snapped, 'What are you saying, *"It's not rocket science?!"* It bloody well is!'

We kept up the watch for another hour, trooping outside at intervals to stamp our feet and mutter darkly.

Then, around 3 a.m., a flurry of excitement. Colonel Worden burst in with an excited astronomer and huddled with Lieutenant Tiffany in a corner. We hung around indiscreetly. The scientists had lost satellite-phone contact with the other half of their party, which was monitoring the shower from a specially constructed camp on the steppe south of town. Had the satellite been knocked out? There was a lot of agitated whispering (from them) and notebook scribbling (from us). Things were looking up.

Half an hour later, one of the team in the field made contact from a telephone in the nearest town. One of their Mongolian colleagues had knocked over a heater and set one of their *ger* headquarters alight. Two Mongolian scientists had sustained minor burns. They would be supplying no more data this night.

Colonel Worden opened his mouth to give us a quote on this development, then thought better of it and marched out.

We sighed and trudged outside for one more look. Still nothing. The US ambassador, defying orders, had gone home. The International School pupils had disappeared. The Mongolian journalists were asleep. My colleague from Beijing wore a deeply pained expression.

At last Colonel Worden came in to face the music, like a trooper. Based on the data they'd gathered so far, he said, clearing his throat, it seemed that the intensity of the meteors was falling off. The cameras were recording between 50 and 100 meteors per hour, and the number was falling. The display had not been the storm, or indeed the shower, that many had predicted. If anyone wanted to leave then, he or she could be dismissed.

'It wasn't a failure, though, because we did have fireballs last night.'

I couldn't believe it. They'd got the date wrong.

I jumped in a jeep with my fellow reporters and the Canadian honorary consul, who gently roused his sleeping driver. We rumbled down the hillside for a moment or two in silence. 'Well, *that* really sucked,' said the diplomat.

When I staggered into work the next day, I asked my bright-eyed colleagues whether they'd stayed up to watch the big show. I wanted someone to share my outrage. But they'd all gone to bed nice and early. No one had – as several of my now rueful expat friends had done – driven out into the countryside in the middle of the night with only a stack of blankets and a bottle of vodka for company. They had not sought an epiphany and had not been disappointed.

'In the countryside, we see shooting stars, all the stars, every night,' said Oyuna. 'And it was very cold last night.'

I had one final conversation with Colonel Worden the next day, just before he and his team boarded their plane and left Mongolia forever. The astronomers wore a slightly sheepish air, but the colonel seemed remarkably chipper. I did not quite have the nerve to suggest that the Leonid experience had been unduly hyped – and disappointed reports were now flowing in from bleary-eyed stargazers from Australia to Japan – in order to gain backing for an expensive information-gathering excursion on behalf of the US military and give a publicity boost to meteor research. But the thought did cross my mind.

In any case, it was clear that, for the colonel, the event had not been a failure at all.

'This is not a bust scientifically. It's a very successful scientific expedition. When you send a weather plane out to survey a hurricane, sometimes the good news is that there is no hurricane. This has provided the data we need to tell our satellite operators that this is not a crisis for them this year.'

I suggested tetchily that they probably knew that by now.

'Look,' said the colonel, 'as an Air Force satellite operator, I'm very pleased. As a scientist, I naturally want to see fireworks in the sky.'

Meteors and asteroids and the like, he explained, were a neglected area of astronomy and one long overdue for a revival – hadn't it been proved, after all, that an asteroid had killed the dinosaurs? The world was just now waking up to the danger posed by space debris.

'We don't understand the phenomenon well enough. Comets are strange things. The consensus in the scientific community,' he said, 'is that we need to study this and build sensors that can find out which ones are threats. We're putting a lot of eggs in satellite baskets; we need to figure out whether we have problems with this sort of phenomenon.' Then, we'd be able – and here I thought I saw his eyes start to gleam – to build weapons capable of destroying an asteroid in space.

For the US military, this sort of study was vital. 'You don't want to confuse a meteor storm with a mobile attack.'

No, I agreed. You don't. Anyway, I said, they must be happy that no satellites had been knocked out by the meteor drizzle.

'I don't want to lose anything,' said the colonel. 'But if they had one that was knocked out for a few hours . . . they might make them tougher.'

The eternal optimist, I thought.

Chapter Sixteen

The Falcon and the Parrot

The Mongolian landscape is a raptor magnet. I was always aware of the presence of large, predatory birds: kites circling in an azure sky, grey fenceposts topped with glaring, immobile hawks. It gave me the creeps. But others reacted differently. Ornithologists, for one – the place was bird heaven to them. I once ran into a gaggle of Belgian birders, flushed with excitement at the prospect of a rough drive in a Russian jeep to the boggy, mosquito-infested shores of a saltwater lake. Other people saw the big birds and thought of cash.

Long ago, someone noticed that birds of prey – fast, accurate and armed to the hilt – are deadly hunting machines. And that humans, slower but bigger and smarter, could force them to hunt for us. Thus, falconry was born. Like so many things, it began as a tool of survival and became a game.

The Mongols of old engaged in falconry, but the practice has largely died out – though the Kazakhs in the west of the country still train huge eagles to hunt for rabbits and other small game. In other countries, the sport survives. In Saudi Arabia and the countries of the Gulf, in particular, it is the sport of kings. The ludicrously rich elite of countries such as Saudi Arabia and Kuwait keep falcon trainers among their retinue and are willing to pay thousands of dollars, American dollars, for a single bird. And they send their emissaries around the world to find them.

Thus, every so often, Saudi or Kuwaiti planes would land at Ulaanbaatar's airport and, a few days or weeks later, would take off again, full of birds in boxes. This is not illegal, at least not in most cases. Although some species of falcon, such as the white gyr falcon, are endangered and thus protected under international agreements such as the Convention on International Trade in Endangered Species, trade in some other varieties of falcon is allowed – although, from an environmental point of view, it may be imprudent.

The Mongolian government, keen to be seen as environmentally aware, stressed that it had placed strict quotas on the number of falcons that could be exported from the country. No one put much faith in the accuracy of its record keeping.

But Mongolia's falcons had a protector, and his name was Parrot. Alan Parrot. He gave it the French pronunciation, but to the Mongolian press – which printed foreign names in the Mongolian style, an initial and a single name – he was always A. Parrot.

He arrived in Mongolia in the autumn and quickly attracted attention. Even among the ragtag band of foreign diplomats, advisors, adventurers, and chancers attracted to this remote country, he stood out: a tall, prodigiously bearded, Caucasian American Sikh, clad from turban to trainers entirely in white. People nudged one another and asked, 'Who is this guy?' They didn't have to wait long for an answer. Soon he began holding press conferences and issuing statements.

His message sounded simple enough: Mongolia's falcon population – its falcon *heritage* – was in danger from greedy businessmen and rapacious politicians who were selling the birds to unscrupulous Middle Eastern traders with no regard for the future of the bird population or for international covenants.

The scion of a wealthy American family, Parrot had, according to his own CV, fallen in love with the regal birds as a teenager. He claimed to have been a falcon trainer to the Shah of Iran. He'd lived in the Arctic, buying falcons from the Inuit. He knew his birds. He was a partner in a company – modestly named Crème de la Crème, Inc. – that specialised (he said) in sustainable falconry and falcon rearing. He had come to Mongolia to make the government an offer he claimed it would be crazy to refuse, a scheme that would combine limited but lucrative sales of mature falcons with scientific research to protect the stock. The sales would generate US$8 million a year – $20,000 per bird – to be split between the Mongolian government and Crème de la Crème. Everyone would win: Parrot, Mongolia, the falcons.

There was just one problem. The government *did* refuse. It declined the Crème de la Crème offer. Mongolia was quite capable of running its own falcon affairs. But Parrot was not a man to take rejection lightly. He was on a *mission*. He increased his barrage of open letters and interviews and stepped up his rhetoric. The Mongolian government, he charged, was complicit in a sinister underground trade in contraband falcons; it was a pawn of an international mafia engaged in a multimillion-dollar trade.

'These birds,' he said at one of his regular press calls, eyes brimming with urgency, 'are like feathered cocaine.'

Nonsense, came the government's reply. The Mongolian authorities were deeply concerned about the country's avian resources and acutely aware of their international obligations. The Ministry of Nature and the Environment had licensed a handful of firms to export a strictly limited number of birds – only 150 in 1997, for example – for a small number of customers, who included the crown prince of Saudi Arabia. The Mongolian government took smuggling very seriously indeed. Why, in a single month, inspectors had arrested 26 poachers.

Parrot was having none of it. In his eyes, the government, by rejecting his offer, had shown its true feathers. 'Mongolia,' he fired back to a roomful of journalists, 'is the epicentre of the world falcon black market.' And this government was incapable of stopping it. 'You don't let an alcoholic work in a liquor store,' he said darkly. The Mongolian journalists waited for the translation, pens quivering, as his translator looked up with an expression of mild panic. I scribbled down the choice quote. This was great stuff.

It got better. The minister of the environment retorted that this was slander and launched a 100-million tugrug – the equivalent of over £70,000 – defamation suit against Alan Parrot.

Parrot hired a Mongolian lawyer and settled in for a long fight. He began to stake out the airport when the Saudi jets landed, watching the boxes of birds being loaded – all perfectly legal, the government said – and haunting the fringes of the action like a snow-white ghost.

He was becoming a media celebrity and was clearly a man comfortable in the spotlight. And we in the media were his co-conspirators: his world of drama and intrigue made excellent copy. His plentiful public pronouncements, simultaneously articulate and rambling, were full of hyperbole and drama. We journalists would sit there as he expounded over the whirr of a dozen tape recorders.

'This,' he said sternly, 'is the most classic case of organised falcon smuggling that has happened in my lifetime. It makes Operation Falcon look like a toy – and Operation Falcon involved simultaneous arrests in Canada, the US, Iceland, France and Germany, with helicopters and SWAT teams surrounding the houses of smugglers. *This is ten times worse.*'

We loved it. Mongolia – in the world of SWAT teams and international crime gangs. I'm sure I wasn't the only reporter in the room who felt a little thrill.

The story had high drama, even if some of the facts were a little hard to come by. No one could say for certain how many falcons were leaving the country or even how many there were to begin with. One census estimated 20,000; another said 1,000.

And, although the media heeded Parrot's cries, the government remained impervious and dismissive. It said little to the press. One of the licensed falcon exporters did, though, appealing to national pride. 'Mongolia was 'advised' for two hundred years by the Manchus and for seventy years by the Russians,' he sneered. 'Now this American wants to tell us what to do.'

But the more they ignored him, the louder Parrot became. He began to make dark intimations of violence. 'I will breathe my last protecting falcons,' he vowed.

Most of us exist amid clamour and confusion, but Parrot lived in a telescopic world. Everything was heightened and intensely focused: him, the falcons, his enemies. These last would be peppered with long, densely argued, vitriolic missives. And the more he was ignored, the longer his list of enemies grew.

His friends – and in the beginning the media were among them – would receive urgent, whispered phone calls. 'It's Alan Parrot. I have some information I think you'll find interesting. My phone is tapped – can you come to my apartment?'

I'd squirm. The wavering heart mistrusts the obsessive. Not that I wasn't interested in his allegations of corruption and intrigue – I emphatically was. Hell, I mostly believed him too. These birds, hard as I found to credit it, were worth huge sums of money. I didn't doubt that people in a cash-hungry nation would be willing to trap and sell them until there wasn't a falcon left from Siberia to the Gobi.

Mongolians talk a great deal about their love of the environment – and it's true. They live off the land, more immediately, more precariously, than you or I. They have a bond with nature, but it is not a sentimental attachment. At best it is a symbiotic relationship. At worst – well, I'd often go for Sunday walks on the Bogd Khan mountain south of Ulaanbaatar. It was a place of steep-sided valleys, twinkling brooks and larch forests, running with rabbits and marmot and deer. It was a Strictly Protected Area, had been a protected forest for more than 200 years – the oldest national park in the world, the government boasted – and its historical and spiritual connections stretched back to the time of Chinggis Khan. On many of my walks, I'd come across loggers cheerfully and unashamedly rolling newly felled trees down the mountainside. Over the months, I saw the park ranger – a friendly man who knew the forest intimately, who'd led me and my friends up the mountain on horseback and pointed out stags and hawks – build himself a fine new log cabin. On one stroll I literally stumbled upon a freshly killed deer, warm blood dripping from a neat bullet hole above its eye.

Falcon poaching was sad but hardly surprising. Still, it was an excellent story. The problem was, he never shut up, this Parrot. I knew what would happen. I'd end up trapped for hours in his flat, squinting at blurrily photocopied documents, an accomplice in his persecuted, self-centred world.

My curiosity got the better of me in the end. I took the bus out to an appropriately Stalinesque high-rise slab near the train station to hear new details of a conspiracy that took in the Mongolian government, the Russian mob and Parrot's rivals in the international world of raptor studies. He didn't let me down. I was treated to a lengthy diatribe against the US ambassador and a leading ornithologist, backed up with sheaves of paper and laced with lashings of paranoia. The government had sent police and immigration officials to his flat to harass him; Russian thugs had started to follow him around; he'd been assaulted by strangers in the market. The falcons, he hinted, were only the wingtips of a much larger conspiracy.

I began to fidget. It all seemed a bit incongruous, there in his flat, which was surprisingly comfortable and homey. The living room contained a big new TV, a comfy sofa, the paraphernalia of yoga and meditation. He took me into the kitchen, with its modern appliances, where he served me a kind of chai he'd brought from the States, raving about it with genuine enthusiasm. It was, I agreed, delicious.

The bedroom door was closed. From behind it came a muffled rustling.

'Um,' I said, inserting myself into a chink in his wall of speech. 'Is there a falcon in there?'

Alan Parrot leaned close. 'This goes no further than this room?'

I nodded.

He pushed open the door. A small falcon flapped out, its regal beauty undercut by its obvious confusion. Parrot stretched out an arm and made soothing noises. Soon the bird was sitting becalmed on his fist, quivering as he stroked it gently with a finger.

'I rescued it from a falcon trader,' he said softly. 'It's far too young and weak to be sold. Once it's strong and healthy enough, I'll let it go. That's why my falcon hospital is so important. There are too many birds like this one.'

In January, Parrot flew out of Mongolia. His lawyer said

Parrot, a diabetic, had gone back to the States to get a fresh supply of insulin. He would return in a few weeks to face his lawsuit and continue the fight.

The weeks stretched into months, with no Parrot on the horizon. 'Flown the coop,' we said to one another. And who could blame him? The falcon flutter died down. Then, one day in June, Oyuna bustled into the office, flushed and excited. 'I've seen Alan Parrot!' she crowed.

The saga was back on.

Only, it wasn't. In Parrot's absence, there had been a change of government. The minister of the environment had lost his job and had subsequently withdrawn his lawsuit. Because he was now a private citizen, he argued, it no longer applied. He had effectively yanked away Parrot's platform. The falconer was not amused and called a press conference to say so. 'It's just a joke, the way he did this,' he scoffed. 'His court case was a private court case – one man against another.'

And the minister had not failed to use the power of government when he sent the police and immigration men around.

'It's as if,' said Parrot, really warming to his subject now, 'I were a private American citizen and I had a court case against another private citizen, and I telephoned the American air force to bomb his house.'

It was good to have him back. And, fortunately, his legal troubles were not quite over. A falcon trader he'd accused of smuggling was suing him for US$50,000. Parrot promised sensational revelations in court.

But the media were losing interest. For months, Parrot

had seemed always to be on the verge of revelation, always just about to deliver the big scoop, to produce the smoking gun. He never quite followed through.

He was also now springing his attacks from dark new alleyways. The American ambassador had become a nemesis – accused of 'obstructing my defence' and subjected to a fusillade of abuse. A British ornithologist who had criticised Parrot's project was dismissed as an accomplice of smugglers. The waters were growing muddier and muddier.

We journalists were collectively backing away. The story was growing old. The momentum had been lost, and other, political scandals now seemed to be more urgent than the fate of a flock of birds.

I was preparing to leave Mongolia, extricating myself from its passions and its crises. And yet . . . I was sure Parrot had a point. The man who was suing him first failed to appear in court and then dropped his lawsuit. More smugglers were caught trying to carry falcons in their luggage onto an Istanbul-bound plane. Mongolia had received a stern letter from the International Wildlife Conservation Law Project in the United States expressing 'doubts the international community has about the rule of wildlife law in Mongolia' after the country was caught exporting protected Argali mountain sheep.

I went to one final press conference, at which Parrot produced a photocopied bank statement showing that a Saudi falcon trader – once arrested in Singapore for smuggling – had withdrawn US$650,000 from a Mongolian bank over a 40-day period. It was the most concrete piece of evidence I'd seen him produce in over a year, but I looked at it with only mild interest. Parrot was unwavering. He'd been pitching his proposal to the Mongolian government for four years; it had been rejected by three different environment ministers. He'd been praised, reviled, stymied and sued.

'Why don't you just give up?' I asked.

'I have an obsessive personality,' he said with certainty. 'I've been told I have quite a bit of Don Quixote in me. It's my nature to pursue things to the end. I just don't give up.

'Falcons are the only thing I have ever done. It's the only thing I know how to do.

'And I will win.'

I'd begun to dread, and tried to avoid, his clandestine phone calls. He caught me one more time, though.

'This is Alan Parrot,' hummed the familiar voice, hauling me out of bed on a Saturday morning. 'I just wanted you to know, they finally got me. Some men broke into my apartment last week. They were Russian. They beat me up and left me lying in my own excrement.'

I thought of something he'd once said: 'If this were Russia, I'd be dead by now.'

'Uh . . .' I wavered.

'I lay there for twenty-four hours until I had enough strength to go to the hospital. I've been there since then; I just got out. These people are serious. They're afraid of me, and they're stepping up their attack. Will you write about this?'

I said something evasive and went back to bed. I did not write about it, did not investigate it, and never spoke to Parrot again. I did see him occasionally on the street in the months before I left Mongolia, still on his private mission. For all I know, he may be there still.

Chapter Seventeen

The Abandoned Monastery

It was another one of those epic Mongolian drives: a dusty town at each end and in between nothing but steppe bleaching into desert. The only landmarks were scattered and temporary: the *gers* and their surrounding flotsam of horses, sheep, goats and two-humped Bactrian camels. The landscape folded our jeep into its rugged contours. Only the double dirt track we were following – fanning out now and again into spaghetti junctions of intertwined tracks – provided evidence that vehicles had passed this way before.

Then, off in a hollow of land, I saw a building: a real building, grey and solid, with a sloping tiled roof. 'Look!' I said, pointing. 'A building!' I wanted confirmation: I feared it was a mirage.

The driver swung the jeep out of the track ruts and bumped across the steppe toward the vision. As we got closer, I could make out the black gaps where the windows should have been; there was no glass to reflect the sunlight. I could see the crumbling walls, the apron of brick and debris around the structure, the tell-tale sloping roof of the main building, the skeletons of smaller outbuildings.

It was a Buddhist monastery, a derelict temple.

We stopped the jeep, and I jumped out eagerly; I love to clamber around abandoned buildings. But this one was not quite abandoned. Around the corner came a very old man, picking his way across the stones. Thin, round-shouldered, wearing a worn, fawn-coloured *del*, clutching the knob of a walking stick with one hand and worrying a string of beads, a Buddhist rosary, with the other.

Chimgee, my guide, greeted him with phrases of the utmost reverence. He said something in a soft rasp of a voice.

'He says won't we come inside for tea? This is his home.'

'His home?' I said, looking with alarm at the sad, neglected structure, half its roof fallen in, all the wood long stripped or rotted away. I would have said no one had lived there for decades.

He led us around the back of the building, where, to my relief, a *ger* sat amid the rubble. Inside, through the gloom and the musty, milky funk, I saw an equally old woman, already putting a pot of water on the dung-fuelled stove.

We sat on the floor, taking care – as I had been instructed – not to point our feet at the hearth. This is considered rude.

The old man sat farthest from the door, as the eldest and the man of the house, and began to speak: quietly, unprompted, telling us his story.

'He was a lama here a long time ago, before the Second World War,' Chimgee translated in an undertone. 'In 1938 soldiers came. They took away the senior lamas, and they chased away the rest, and they smashed and burned the monastery so the lamas could not return.

'He ran away, buried his lama's robes and beads and

other things, and became a herder. But a few years ago, after the democratic changes, he came back here, to watch over what is left of the monastery. He hopes one day it will be restored, but now there is no money and no interest.'

'And the robes? The religious icons? Did he dig them up again?'

The old man shook his head.

'It was a long time ago. He has forgotten where they are.'

It was a story I heard again and again. Before the Communist revolution, Mongolia had hundreds of Buddhist monasteries and more than 100,000 monks. By the end of the Communist period, there was one functioning monastery and perhaps a couple of hundred monks. Once again, it seemed, seven decades had comprehensively undone the work of 700 years.

Buddhism in Mongolia layered itself on to a much older faith: the mystical shamanism, which worshipped the spirits in the earth, the water and especially the vast blue sky. The Mongol conquests of the thirteenth century brought the Mongol soldiers and their kings into contact with people from other faiths: Buddhists from Tibet, Taoists from China, Muslims and Christians from farther afield. The Mongol khans were a religiously open-minded lot who welcomed representatives of the various faiths to their court; Khubilai Khan famously invited them to debate in front of him to try to convert the khan. But although he employed Buddhist advisors and had respect for the religion's teachings, neither he nor his successors made Buddhism a state religion.

It was Altan Khan, the sixteenth-century ruler of the rump of the Mongol Empire, who became Mongolia's first Buddhist ruler and promoted Buddhism as a national religion, a way to unify – and perhaps to pacify – the fractious Mongol people.

It worked. It worked so well that by the turn of the century the monasteries were the richest, most important and most influential institutions in a threadbare, underpopulated nation. They held large chunks of the land and much of the learning. And their power was secular as well as spiritual. By the first decades of the twentieth century, 100,000 men – a third of the adult male population – were monks; monasteries controlled a fifth of the country's land and ruled over several hundred thousand people. There were 140 Living Buddhas – feudal rulers-cum-priests, regarded as semidivine – with the Bogd Khan, Mongolia's holy king, at the top.

The Bogd Khan was not a simple cleric. He crammed his palace with motor cars, stuffed carcasses of exotic animals, riches and trinkets from many lands. His appetite for food, drink and women was legendary. None of the outside observers who met him came away impressed; to foreign eyes, the Buddhist clergy seemed to be an indolent, degenerate elite.

But many Mongolians were loyal to the church; it provided the only infrastructure the country had. When Chinese rule collapsed, the religious establishment filled the void, and the Bogd Khan became Mongolia's secular as well as its religious leader.

When a small band of rebels with Soviet backing took power in 1921, they looked warily at the wealth and power of the religious establishment. At first, perhaps, they hoped that the power of the church would wither of its own accord; when the Bogd Khan died three years later, no reincarnation was named. But the monasteries remained rich and powerful. The Communists at first tried to strike an accommodation; when it failed – in moves that exactly mirrored Stalin's policies in the Soviet Union – they turned to persecution. The monasteries were stripped of their power: taxed, forbidden to teach or recruit children. The founding of new monasteries was forbidden, and monks lost their exemption from military service.

But all this was not enough. By 1934, there were still 3,000 temples in Mongolia, and the church's annual income was almost equal to that of the state. Monasteries were appropriated by the government and the monks turned out; several times, lamas staged armed uprisings. Things were getting ugly.

The conflict reached its peak in 1937 and 1938. With Mongolia facing the threat of a Japanese invasion, the government got serious. Something like 2,000 high-ranking monks were executed, and many others were sent to Siberia or jailed. The monasteries were closed or destroyed. It's hard to know the exact scale of the purge. The respected Mongolist Morris Rossabi cites a 'conservative estimate' of 35,000 people killed or imprisoned between 1930 and 1950, a figure that takes in both religious and political purges. Others estimate that as many as 100,000 'enemies of the state' were killed.

Only one temple – the vast Gandan Monastery in Ulaanbaatar – was allowed to remain open, occupied by 100 carefully schooled monks, as a tourist attraction, museum and showpiece of the Communists' religious tolerance.

Mongolians no longer went to the church for education or succour; in its place, gradually, they got kindergartens, schools, nationalised health care, the chance to attend university. Some people felt the loss of their religious traditions deeply and continued to worship in private. With time, though, feelings subsided, and many came to believe the trade-off was an acceptable one. Younger Mongolians, born and raised in an officially atheist Communist state, knew no other system.

With time, much of the passion drained from the issue, and religion became less of a threat to the authorities. Gandan's monks were allowed to travel and to build links with Buddhists in other Asian countries; by the late 1970s, the Dalai Lama was even permitted to travel to Mongolia. The authorities could point to this as proof that religious freedom – enshrined in the 1960 Constitution – really did flourish in Mongolia.

Now, of course, it's all different. When the Russians left and the Communists softened and crumpled, some of the old monks emerged from their civilian disguises, donned their gold and maroon robes, dusted off the sutras they'd lovingly tended in secret, and returned to the few monasteries that remained standing, to await the religious revival.

Only, it didn't come. Not really. Of course, the monks are now free to worship openly, to play a part in civic life, to teach young novices. They have received visits from the two most famous figures of Tibetan Buddhism – the Dalai Lama and Richard Gere. Mongolians once again visit the temples. But it is only the old, with their beads and their stillness and quiet, who look devout. The young couples who go to Gandan to wander through the cool, incense-scented buildings and admire the giant golden Buddha, or the children giving the prayer wheels a spin – they wear the expressions of tourists.

'What about you?' I asked Chimgee – young, city raised, university educated – as we drove away from the old couple in their *ger* by the ruined temple. 'Do you believe?'

She thought about it for a long moment. 'I don't know. I'm not really religious. But I do think that, if I have some problem, I can ask Buddha, and he will help me.'

I think most people of her age felt the same way. They respected their culture and the faith of their ancestors, but it did not play a large part in their daily lives. A genuine revival of the faith in Mongolia – well, that takes money, for a start. Some restoration has been done. There are now perhaps 150 functioning monasteries in the country, most of them small and spartan. A gleaming new golden Buddha has been installed at Gandan to replace the original, which was stolen and reportedly melted down by Stalin's troops. But many people believe there are more pressing issues, and Mongolia just does not have the money for the sweeping restoration and aggressive proselytising that would be needed for a wide-scale religious revival.

Another religion does, though.

Squeezing into Pizza de la Casa one day, I shouldered up to the counter beside two young Americans wearing black shoes, black trousers, white shirts and lapel badges. 'Elder Johnson' said one badge. 'Elder Roberts' said the other.

'What do you do in Mongolia?' asked the Mongolian student behind the counter, eager as ever to practise his English.

'Well,' said the blond-haired, acne-spotted one, 'we tell people we're English teachers, because the Mongolian government says we have to say that. But really we're missionaries.'

'Have you found the Lord?' chimed in the tanned, brown-haired one.

Christian missionaries were everywhere in Mongolia. And I mean everywhere. Not just the Mormons, who travelled in pairs and were unflaggingly polite and easily identifiable. Every provincial capital, and many smaller towns, had a resident family – usually American but sometimes German or even Finnish – of a beaming couple and 2.4 towheaded children: teaching English, holding Bible classes and church services. They were backed by congregations at home, and they had money – money to produce Mongolian-language Bibles and religious comics and glossy videos of the life of Christ.

Money to fund a Mongolian-American TV station, Eagle TV, which slipped in Bible quotes and religious cartoons between its broadcasts of Mongolian news and American sports. Money to send young Mongolian converts on scholarships to small colleges in Tennessee or to Brigham Young University in Utah.

No surprise – it worked. Although the media often railed against the pernicious influence of the missionaries, the government – desperate for English teachers and for foreign funds – tolerated them. I found a country in which Christianity was a glamour religion, one for the young and aspirational. The staffs of development agencies and international organisations were full of young Christians, because they tended to be educated, intelligent, presentable and speak excellent English.

'We've hired a new translator,' said my friend Rob, who worked for an international environmental project. 'His English is terrific, and he works really hard, but I think I have to fire him.'

'How come?'

'It's the praying. He prays in the office – out loud. All the time. It's driving everybody crazy.'

I, too, had worked for a time with a young Mongolian Christian. He was bright and earnest and punctual – but he had that fervid inner peace of the convert, and it made me nervous. He would sidle up to Mongolian colleagues and casually introduce Jesus into the conversation. And his theology was, shall I say, limited – I could not persuade him, for example, that Catholics were Christian.

All these Christians made me uneasy, so it was with a sense of relief that I read an article in a Mongolian newspaper headlined 'I WAS A FAKE CHRISTIAN.' The subject, a young man in his twenties, gleefully described how he had pretended to believe in Jesus in order to reap the benefits of Christian largesse.

'First I got involved with some Russian missionaries, and they sent me to Russia to study. Then I joined some Americans, and I got to go to a college in the United States. I've learned to speak Russian and English – and I don't believe any of it!'

That made me feel a lot better, I can tell you.

Chapter Eighteen

How the Mongolians Got Their Names Back

I met a man with a passion for names. He was slight, soft-spoken and balding. He sat in a big, barely furnished office and showed me his life's work: a list of names, hundreds of them, running down the pages of a cheaply bound, coarse-papered book.

His hand skimmed gently over the surface of the paper. He'd spent years compiling this list. These weren't just any names; they were Mongolia's lost surnames.

His own name was Serjee, and I'd first heard of him through a small item in the bottom corner of a Mongolian newspaper. It reported that the Mongolian government was planning to introduce modern plastic identity cards to replace the old paper domestic passports that all Mongolians carried. For the new ID cards, all Mongolians would have to provide, in addition to date and place of birth, three names: their given name, their father's name and their family name.

'But Mongolians don't have family names,' I protested to my colleagues. Mongolians are basically single-name people. I'd often seen them get confused about how to fill in foreign forms – what should they put in the box marked 'Surname'? 'You use your given name and your father's name.'

It had taken me a while to get used to this. Mongolians effectively have only one, given name. Lovely, meaningful names, too, usually bestowed with great care and forethought, often compounds of two words to give a strong, bright clarity: Sukhbaatar, axe hero; Narantsetseg, sunflower; Bolormaa, crystal mother; or – my favourite – Bayarsaikhan, which translates into English as happy holiday.

On official documents and for purposes of identification, they add their father's name; in common practice, it's reduced to an initial. So Bold's son Ganbat is B. Ganbat, and Ganbat's daughter Delgermaa would be G. Delgermaa. It's the kind of system that can only work in countries with a small, relatively homogeneous population: Mongolia, say, or Iceland.

A few months earlier, I'd read about how some politician had proposed the idea of introducing European-style surnames that would be passed on through the generations. It was a modernising move that would bring Mongolia into line with international practice, he'd argued. And wouldn't it be gratifying if your grandchildren could share your name?

The proposal didn't get very far. Most of the 76 MPs – among them multiple Batbayars, two Ganbolds and a brace of Ganhuyags – were content with the status quo. And some just couldn't get their heads around the idea.

'How can your grandchildren have your name if you're not their father?' scoffed one Communist deputy. 'If you want to give them your name, you'll have to adopt them first.'

You couldn't really argue with that. But now Oyuna was telling me that the idea wasn't as foreign to Mongolian practice as I'd assumed.

'We used to have family names,' she told me. 'In the

feudal times. Under Communism, we stopped. It was because you could tell from someone's family name if they were from the nobility.'

'So do you know what your family name is?'

'I do,' she said with pride, 'because we were once a very distinguished family. My father kept a book, a family tree, which his father had kept before him. But I think many people have forgotten.'

Intrigued, I did a quick office survey. Who knew their family name?

'Nope,' said Zaya.

'Sorry,' said Bat-Erdene.

'I haven't got a clue,' admitted Jargal.

I scuttled back to Oyuna. 'No one knows their family name, and it says here the ID cards are going to be issued starting next month. Nobody here has filled out an application. Isn't this a bit of a problem?'

She, too, failed to look concerned. 'There's a man mentioned in this article, a Serjee. It says he has made a list of all Mongolians' family names. You should speak to him.'

Serjee worked at the Central Library, a big yellow building constructed in the Soviet colonial style. To enter it, you walked up a flight of broad steps, through pillars, and past the empty space where Stalin's statue had stood until it was taken down and hauled away in 1990; then you stood, game-show-like, in front of a row of doors trying to guess which one among them would be open; once you'd figured it out by the process of elimination, it slammed shut behind you with a crack that set papers rattling, shelves shaking and scholars leaping throughout the building.

The interior of the library was musty and underlit, with a grand and creaky staircase running up the middle. Serjee's office was at the top of the stairs. Serjee sat behind a wooden desk adorned with a blotter and a black bakelite telephone. He handed me his business card, which was oddly garish – pink and glossy, with a golden *soyombo*, the national emblem, in the top left corner. 'Director, State Central Library of Mongolia,' it said.

'Historical documents show that Mongolians have used family names since at least the eighth century,' he told me. '*The Secret History of the Mongols*, our ancient national history, is full of examples.

'Someone from one area or tribe would become famous, in war for example, and others would take his name.'

Gradually this grew into a system of clan names, reflecting – like English surnames – an ancestor's profession, military prowess or quirk. The keeping of family records was taken seriously in feudal Mongolian society; many families, like Oyuna's, kept books detailing their family tree. Nobles and khans had their own official registrars.

'It was forbidden,' Serjee recounted, 'to marry anyone who, tracing back seven generations, appeared on the same family tree as you.'

That was a useful idea, I thought – a buffer against inbreeding in a tiny population and a spur to interclan alliances in a fractious society. Family names were part of the stitch work that knit together Mongolian society.

The 'people's revolution' ripped apart that fabric and sewed it together in a new pattern.

'After the 1924 revolution, the authorities decided to destroy genealogical trees, in order to destroy the titles and political power of the nobility,' Serjee continued. The record books, often tracing families back for centuries, were ordered destroyed, and Mongolians were instructed to use only the father's name on official records.

I didn't know whether to be comforted or horrified by the fact that, once again, seven decades had sufficed to undo the legacy of seven centuries. I told Serjee the results of my straw poll – only one person in six I'd asked had known his or her family name.

He nodded, unsurprised. 'We think about 60 per cent of Mongolians do not know their family names. But all that will change.'

Just then the old black phone rang – a loud, shrill stage ring. Serjee picked it up and had a quick rustle of conversation. He put it down and turned back to me with an apology. 'That was a member of parliament. They're all phoning me now, asking me what their name is.'

'You're the keeper of the names?'

'You could say that. In 1990, when things were changing, parliament began to discuss reintroducing family names. In 1991, the president officially supported the idea. It was popular – people wanted to know more about their culture and their history.'

So the Mongolian Academy of Sciences assembled a reconnaissance team. Serjee and a handful of other academics and officials with an interest in genealogy fanned out across the country. For five years, and in addition to holding down day jobs, they sat in dank local government offices digging through dusty archives, and they talked to old people.

The result was the book, listing more than 1,300 names catalogued by area – 50 to 60 for every *soum*, the equivalent of a county, in Mongolia. Serjee looked at the names fondly. The book, he explained, was designed to help Mongolians in tracing their own family names. The rest was up to them. The reintroduction of family names would require a sort of national pilgrimage. 'People from your own area will probably know something about your family,' Serjee said. 'You should go there and ask them, especially the old people, about your parents and your grandparents.'

I was trying to take this in. He was suggesting a participatory history project involving every adult in the country, an endeavour almost biblical in scope. Surely this was one of the most ambitious genealogical projects ever undertaken? Hundreds of thousands of people were being asked to rediscover their roots, to recover long-submerged identities.

It would be impossible almost anywhere else, in any land where technology, migration and upheaval had withered the links binding countryside to city and generation to generation. I couldn't believe it possible, even in Mongolia. It seemed to be another example of what, depending on my mood, I thought of as Mongolians' endearing blindness to obstacles or their infuriating naivety. I could think of all sorts of obstacles to its realisation: money, logistics, lethargy, ignorance. What about city dwellers who knew nothing of their grandparents and rural life? What about orphans, for God's sake?

Serjee was not flustered. 'I think there are very few Mongolians who know nothing of their mother and father. A few street children, perhaps. But of course it is different in the city than in the countryside, and we can't neglect people who don't know about their family names. So we decided they can select a new name. For example, if no one knows about my name, but I know my parents came from Galt *soum*, I can select one of the names from that area.

'And,' he added casually, 'people can invent names if they like.'

What, anything? I asked. Yes, he said – though of course the family name of Chinggis Khan was off-limits.

'But what if someone chooses it?'

He looked offended at the idea. 'Mongolians are honest! They respect their fathers and grandfathers. They would never do that.'

He seemed to be so certain the plan would work. 'Many Mongolians will be getting new names. It's new and strange now, but after three or four generations it will be a real family, with its own name, distinct from other families.'

There was a tone in his voice I'd heard before – a slight yearning for something; for stability, perhaps, or continuity. 'That's important, is it?' I asked.

'It's very important to know about your family,' he said. 'Every family has things it wants to pass on to the next generation.'

I wasn't sure about the rest of the country, but Serjee's low-key enthusiasm had worked on me. I left with a warm glow. I was ready to rush out and interview my own grandparents, to look again at the family tree they'd compiled tracing our roots back to the old country.

I hailed a car in the street. 'Hey,' I said to the driver, sticking my head over the top of the front seat. 'Do you know your family name?'

'No,' he said. 'You don't need to know it in everyday life, do you?'

Had he heard about the names project?

'News to me,' he said.

Undeterred, I tried a woman in the street.

'I read something about it in the paper,' she nodded. 'I don't know my own family name, but I'll definitely try to find out. I'll find time to look at the book and to ask my family. It's a good idea, isn't it? We don't know enough about our history and our traditions.'

This was the reaction I usually got – passive support. People meant to look up their roots, approved of the idea in principle. But few people had got around to doing anything about it just yet, and the deadline was only weeks away. I began to panic on their behalf.

The next week, the government announced that the introduction of the new ID cards would have to be delayed. There wasn't enough money in the budget. Economics triumphed over history once again. More than a year later, Mongolians finally began to receive their new ID cards. Contrary to Serjee's prediction, early indications were that more than half the population had chosen Borjigin – Chinggis Khan's tribal name.

Chapter Nineteen

The Border

'This is *bull*shit,' moaned Michael, and his Caterpillar boot stamped up a little flurry of Mongolian dust.

We'd been kicking our heels in the parched frontier town for two days. All we wanted was to get out.

The teenage soldier in the guardhouse eyed us shyly. Batkhisheg, our friendly but flustered government minder, shrugged apologetically. 'It is impossible,' she said, with quiet finality. 'No foreigners are allowed to go to the border. There is,' she explained helpfully, 'a problem with cattle rustlers.'

'I *know*,' I whined. 'That's why we came.'

We hadn't foreseen this back in Ulaanbaatar, when Michael and I, with the originality so common among journalists, simultaneously hit upon the same story idea. We'd both noticed the reports that popped up in the papers every week or two, filed from the remote province of Uvs, nearly 930 miles west of the capital: stories of armed gangs on horseback sweeping over the border from the Russian Republic of Tuva, seizing livestock from hapless Mongolian herders, then galloping back across the frontier.

Many of the stories were laced with violence and gunplay. In one raid, bandits had shot a horse out from under a pursuing Mongolian border guard. A member of parliament who had visited the area spoke of residents cowering in a 'state of war.'

For Michael, a young Californian stringer nurtured

on Paul Theroux and *Outside* magazine, it was irresistible. And I, too, wanted to go to that border. If possible, I wanted to go to Tuva, a mountain-cupped, and apparently rustler-riven, pocket of the Russian Federation – a land even more mistily remote and thrillingly obscure than Mongolia.

Michael and I agreed to travel together. The provincial capital, Ulaangom – Red Sand – was a bumpy four-hour flight from Ulaanbaatar on a wheezing, propeller-driven Antonov. I passed the time trying to prevent myself from counting the number of people squeezed into the plane's 47 fraying seats (I stopped at 60). Michael threw up over his copy of *Riding the Iron Rooster*. At last the plane shuddered to a halt on a dusty airstrip and coughed up its cargo of big families, oversized bags, large appliances and small animals.

Ulaangom was everything I'd hoped for in a wild-west border town: raked by dust and by horses that trotted down the long main street and across the windswept square; dotted with pairs of sunburned herders exchanging snuff bottles; haunted by rings of raptors circling above the ramshackle market.

We checked into the local hotel, which was better than the Mongolian average: the rooms were clean, the shower cold, the mutton hot and the beer warm – but at least there *was* beer.

When we presented ourselves as journalists at the slab of concrete that housed the governor's office, everyone was very helpful. Of course we could go to the border. A jeep would be available in the morning. Batkhisheg – the governor's grandly titled international relations officer (her contribution to international relations appeared to involve playing a lot of solitaire on the computer) – would be our guide. There was just the formality of getting a permit from the border army.

My heart sank at that. Armies, I have noticed, are rarely an aid to one's travel plans.

And so it proved. The commander of the local frontier detachment said that we had, alas, come at a very sensitive time. Extra troops had been shipped in from Ulaanbaatar in response to the cattle-rustling epidemic. Manoeuvres were under way. Roadblocks had been set up. The border was strictly out of bounds.

Futilely Michael and I protested. We bullied. We phoned our superiors in Ulaanbaatar, who promised to phone people who knew people in the Ministry of Defence. We sulked. We were, in the nicest way possible, ignored.

I was crushed. I hadn't really thought we'd be allowed to cross the border, but I had imagined us sitting down for a bowl of salty milk tea with a platoon of border guards while they told us hair-raising stories of night raids and horseback pursuits. Michael confessed that he'd indulged in vivid fantasies set to a soundtrack of bullets pinging off jeep doors.

To cheer ourselves up, we dropped in on the province's police chief, a polite, burly man who was happy to fill us in on the region's spiralling cattle-theft rate. 'Thieves used to steal cattle in summer, when they were fat,' he explained. 'But now it is no longer dependent on the season. Last year there were 38 cases in which 839 cattle were stolen from Tuva. We solved

18 incidents and recovered 420 cattle. From Uvs, there were 76 cases of theft involving 1,630 animals. Only 289 were recovered.'

The problem had been growing steadily worse over the past decade, he said. And once the livestock had been spirited into the forested mountain valleys of Tuva, there was little the Mongolian police could do about it. 'When cattle are stolen, the Russian and Mongolian soldiers negotiate; *then* they tell the police,' he sighed. 'But after a few days, the animals have already been turned into meat.'

We raised the question of firearms.

Evidently missing the note of hope in our voices, he set about allaying our fears. 'People don't usually get shot – usually they get beaten,' he said. He must have sensed our disappointment, because he added, 'One time, a guy got his ear cut off. And another one was burned with hot metal.'

He looked at us with a touch of anxiety. Hospitable Mongolian that he was, he wanted us to go away from the interview happy. We assured him that he'd been most helpful.

Prickling with excitement and frustration, Michael and I passed the evening wandering up and down the main street, where we soon attracted a circle of curious residents. Were there many sheep in our country? Was winter cold there? Oh, yes, I assured them, shooting a smug Canadian look at Michael – in *my* homeland, but not in his. The Mongolians and I spent a moment gazing at Michael with sympathy and pity.

This northern bond established, we moved on to

cultural common ground. 'Schwarzenegger *sain*!' – Arnie's great! – I found myself agreeing with one friendly young film fan. He took this as a signal to launch into a passionate explanation of Arnold's superiority over Van Damme; my limited Mongolian stumbled at the conversational challenge, and we wished our new friends goodnight.

We went back to the hotel, ate mutton and rice, drank tepid Russian beer, and chatted with the only other foreign guest, a frazzled young French ornithologist whose expedition across western Mongolia – in the sidecar of a Russian motorbike driven by a hunky young Mongolian – had foundered. They were having engine problems, she told us.

Us too, we said.

In the morning, we made one last foray. We strode into Batkhisheg's office with an air of determination and a map of Mongolia, which we spread out on the desk. 'We'd like to go here,' we said, pointing to the wonderfully named town of Salt (Davst), which sat beside a large inland sea called Uvs Lake. We had heard of the lake's famed bird life, we told her (so we had – from the young Frenchwoman the night before), and wanted to see for ourselves.

Batkhisheg was not fooled. 'But that is beside the border,' she said.

'What about here?' I pointed to a nearby town.

She shook her head.

'Here?' I stabbed at a village named Turgen, about halfway between Ulaangom and the border.

'Oh, yes, you can go there. It is not beside the border.'

'How far from the border is it?' asked Michael.

'Perhaps 20 miles.'

'Are there herders there who have had livestock stolen by rustlers?'

'Oh, yes.'

We were on the road.

Turgen was a typically ramshackle small Mongolian town: a couple of simple wooden municipal buildings, a few rows of cupcake-shaped *gers* behind sagging fences. But it lay in a beautiful setting, on a grassy plain in the shadow of a range of snow-capped mountains.

Batkhisheg popped into the town hall to look for the local governor. She received directions, and we set off in the jeep. After stopping and asking at several *gers*, we pulled up at one where we were greeted by a shirtless man surrounded by small children. He was introduced as Byambaa, the head of the local council.

He nodded slowly when he heard what we were after. 'In the last two years, herders from our *soum* have lost about 100 horses to thieves,' he said. 'Some of the thieves are Tuvans, and some are Mongolians who steal the animals and pass them on to Tuvan handlers. We told the Tuvan police, but the horses were never found.

'We're planning to have a meeting with the provincial government, police and army to discuss the problem. But what we really need is to invite the Tuvan president here. Many people think this. The problem will only be resolved by a contract.'

I was surprised by the suggestion that the Tuvan head of state be invited to sit down and negotiate – in all likelihood, given Mongolian hospitality, literally over tea. I had expected – indeed, rather hoped for – more animosity. We asked Byambaa, none too subtly, if he bore a grudge against the Tuvans.

'On the whole, Tuvan-Mongolian relations are going quite well,' he said evenly. 'We understand one another. But some people continue to steal animals, because they are poor and want to be rich.'

So they were making some poor people poorer. People such as Sambuu, a herder whom Byambaa took us to meet. Sambuu's *ger* was perched on the mountainside above the village; Sambuu had a magnificent view over the plain to the blue slash of Uvs Lake. But he was clearly not enjoying it.

In midafternoon, his *ger* was engulfed by the shadow of the mountain. Sambuu sat alone in the gloom and spoke in a whisper. 'The thieves came in the night, on the 23rd of April,' he murmured. 'They stole my horses – twenty-six in all.'

'Did that cause you much difficulty?' I asked.

Sambuu shot me a puzzled look, as if the question were too obvious to warrant a response. 'It's very difficult,' he enunciated slowly, as if to an idiot. 'I can't herd my cows and goats. I have to walk.'

We kept prodding. Did he hate the Tuvans? Would he move farther away from the border zone?

'Perhaps the thieves were Mongolians – who can say? And I'll stay here. This is my homeland. All my family are here.'

Back in Ulaangom, we had heard a similar sense of place from Norov, the veteran local correspondent for the state-owned news agency (and, it turned out, the originator of all those reports that had intrigued us back in Ulaanbaatar).

Western people were proud of their regional traditions, he said, such as their oversized *gers* – much bigger around than the central Mongolian variety – and their descent from one of several minority ethnic groups: Dorvod, Bayad, Kazakh. In a country where the majority group, Khalkh Mongols, makes up 85 per cent of the population, the west is a veritable cultural mosaic.

Ironically, the collapse of Communism at the start of the 1990s had done more to attack the region's local pride and identity than had seven decades of Stalinist rule. The Communists had been unwilling or unable to stop the movement of these nomadic people, Mongolian and Tuvan, back and forth across the border separating two obscure, half-wild outposts of the socialist world. It was Mongolia's move to democracy, and the government's attempts to assert national independence, that cut western Mongolians off from their Tuvan friends and neighbours.

We had expected to hear bitterness against the Tuvans. Instead, we found a quiet yearning.

'People who live near the border know each other very well,' explained Norov over dinner one night. 'Often they are even related. One area in Tuva is populated by people who speak the Mongolian language, and many Mongolians who live near the border can speak Tuvan.

'Until ten years ago, the border was open. Life was good then. Nowadays, people who want to visit Tuva have to get a visa from the Russian embassy in Ulaanbaatar. It's a big problem for people's lives.'

'Before 1990, livestock theft was only a small problem, because people could move freely across the border, depending on pasture,' the police chief had told us. 'Until a few years ago, there was friendship across the border. In 1990, they began to put up border guards, and that's when the cattle theft began in earnest.'

The solution, everyone agreed, was to reopen the border. But there's little chance of that. The government in faraway Ulaanbaatar has responded to the crime wave with a promise to beef up border security. No one holds much stock in this pledge. The border army is composed mainly of underfed and ill-equipped teenage conscripts from families too poor to buy their sons out of military service. Soldiers complain that their broken-down vehicles are easily outrun by a man on a fast horse.

We left Sambuu on his lonely hillside and, after some all-star whining from me and Michael, pushed on toward the border. The Russian jeep heaved its way across an epically stark landscape: a rolling sea of grass – still dusty brown, though it was May – spiked around the rim with granite thrusts of mountain. Every few miles we'd pass a little outpost of humanity: a *ger* or two, a herd of sheep and goats swirling around a stout herder on horseback.

At the top of a pass, we stopped at an *ovoo* – a pyramid of stones topped with scraps of blue silk that serves as a landmark and an outdoor shrine to the gods of earth and sky – to chat with a family of nomads moving house. They led a row of camels, which plodded sullenly under the clan's possessions: cooking stove, chests of drawers, the rolls of felt and folding latticework walls and round roof hole that made up their *ger*. A couple of toddlers ogled us from bouncing, camel-slung baskets.

'Nice day,' we said, more or less.

One young man got down from the camel he was riding and lit a filterless cigarette.

We had been in Mongolia long enough to know what to do. We talked about the weather. How was the spring?

'Bad,' he said. 'It's too dry. It hasn't rained yet this year.' His family was moving to the lake for the summer. There their parched animals would at least have water.

Everyone we met in Uvs complained about the drought. It was the driest spring in years.

Mongolian nomads have nothing but their animals; that's why cattle theft is among the worst of crimes. They rarely even have fodder to feed their herds. When a winter is too cold, or a spring too dry, thousands of dead animals will make a feast for vultures on the steppe, and herding families will go hungry.

Capitalism has not changed this. Indeed, the collapse of Communism has made things worse in remote rural areas as the market has concentrated economic activity around Ulaanbaatar, at the epicentre of Mongolia's handful of paved roads and its single rail line. Hundreds of families – and thousands of animals – leave Uvs every year. And every year it gets worse.

The drought and the poverty were exactly the same a few miles away in Tuva, as everyone in these parts knew. It dawned on me that no one, apart from me and

Michael, thought the idea of Tuvan cattle rustlers the least bit exotic.

'There aren't so many livestock in Tuva now,' Norov had shrugged. 'People are poor.'

Now the camel herder shrugged, too, when we asked him how he felt about the rustlers. He'd seen the army roadblock that'd been set up on the road just here until yesterday (at this Batkhisheg shot me and Michael a reproachful look), but what could he do? It was a threat, like the drought, that he was powerless to control.

Leaving the camel train behind, we egged Batkhisheg on a bit farther. Purely sightseeing, we promised. We weren't kidding. There was a place called Uureg Lake; I'd heard it was spectacular. And so it proved: a cool turquoise pool in a mat of stiff brown grass and purple irises. On the far side, in a light mist, was a range of white-capped peaks.

'Tuva,' said Batkhisheg, in a tone that said, will that shut them up?

It did. As Batkhisheg squirmed a little, nervously, Michael and I took pictures of our foreign-correspondent Shangri-La. Then Michael discovered an urge to fish and spent a happy hour getting tangled in his hand line. I sat on a rock and inhaled the tangy air and the serenity; I also felt the dark and the chill creeping in, and I began to hear sounds. It was as lovely and lonely a spot as I have ever seen. I wouldn't have wanted to be alone there; and I wouldn't have wanted, in the long nights, for my friends across the lake to be turned into strangers.

Then we let a relieved Batkhisheg bundle us into the jeep, and we headed back to Ulaangom.

The border may be closed, but we did meet one Tuvan before we returned to Ulaanbaatar. He was in Ulaangom jail, where, the warden informed us, 80 of the 105 prisoners were serving sentences for livestock theft.

Nachan, a 22-year-old Tuvan, was not one of them. He was a rail-thin young man covered in a film of dust, from his shaved head to his bare brown feet. I would not have been able to tell him from a Mongolian, except that he spoke Russian.

But before he spoke, he opened his mouth and emitted an extraordinary sound, or layers of sound, a vibrating moan on top of a rumbling growl. The notes hovered, rose, dipped and rolled, an eerie web of melody, before retreating back down his throat.

'That was a Tuvan national song about the beautiful River Tes, which flows into Uvs Lake,' he explained, while we sat, gently vibrating. 'I've been throat singing since I was ten. My voice was really good; I gave a lot of concerts, and I taught others as well. But last winter I got a sore throat, and after that it wasn't so good.'

Then the warden gave him a bowl of water to clear his throat, and he told us his story. 'My parents are herders, and one day twelve of our cows were stolen, along with two horses. My parents herded those cattle for a living. My mother cried when they were stolen. I was really sad too. The milk is very good for us.

'My father, brother and I went to find our animals. We didn't know where the border was – it wasn't marked. Suddenly some soldiers came and arrested us.

That's when we knew we were in Mongolia. I got six months for crossing the border illegally. My brother got a year, and my father 18 months.

'We never did find our animals. But after we were sent to jail, an old Mongolian man came to see us. He said he wanted to help us, because long ago there was no border, and Mongolians and Tuvans were friends. He said he had been friends with my grandfather, and he would help us get our animals back.'

Then he shook us each by the hand, the warden patted him on the shoulder, and he strolled back to rejoin his work detail.

Six months later, after I had left Mongolia, I heard that the cattle-rustling problem had grown even worse. Two herders, a husband and wife living near the Tuvan border, had died from multiple gunshot wounds when their *ger* was attacked by a band of five cattle thieves. Their son was shot in the hands and legs but survived. The rustlers made off with 68 cows and two horses.

The Mongolian government filed a note of protest with the Russian Embassy in Ulaanbaatar, accusing Russian frontier guards and the Russian government of ignoring the cross-border problem. Russian police reported that they had arrested five men in connection with the crime; one committed suicide while in detention.

'Transborder livestock theft cases are becoming more common and cruel,' warned a Mongolian foreign ministry official.

Chapter Twenty

The End of the Line

It's an odd thing. In Mongolia, you spend so much time dreaming of things you could have if you were elsewhere – Szechuan chicken with peanuts, reliable hot water, Big Macs. Of countries with fewer raw noses, fewer sharp edges.

But then you find yourself standing at a railway station in the bright unblinking light of an Ulaanbaatar morning, watching the great green diesel-driven Moscow-Beijing express heave up to the platform, being bustled toward the train on a tide of Mongolians and their mounds of luggage – so much luggage! – and you find yourself resisting.

At least I did. I felt a sudden and unaccountable surge of panic, an urge to fight my way back through the throng and walk away from the train, through the station, and out to the street, to flag down a passing Volga, sink into its capacious seat, and ask the driver to take me through the dusty, bedraggled city to Apartment 42, Building 1, 12th Microdistrict. Home.

I didn't, of course. My home, surely, was elsewhere. I got on the train, heaved my bags onto a bunk in one of the compact compartments, then stood by the window and watched the city roll by for the last time. It didn't take long – past the ragged children scavenging coal by the railway tracks; past the smokestacks of the power station and the backs of neglected factories; a glimpse of the square and of the park with its battered old Ferris wheel; past soot-encrusted *ger* districts that tapered to scattered homesteads and a few folk watering their cattle by the river; and then the open countryside.

The train snaked through the hills that surround the city, through a landscape, now in summer, a rich, heart-stopping green. Then the hills fell away, and the land settled to level, and the train tracks snapped into a straight line: a band of steel, pointing to China.

For a long stretch, it was a land whose bottom was green and whose top was blue and on which there were no landmarks larger than a cow. You could imagine it a land without people. It was a landscape excellently suited to contemplation and melancholy.

Even I couldn't keep that up forever, though. This train was my home for the next 30 hours; I'd better go and join it. This was, after all, a Mongolian community – the last I'd find myself in for some time, maybe forever. There were more Mongolians on the train than we'd passed in a hundred miles.

So I did what you have to do if you really want to become part of the community of travellers, to join the rolling stock. I went to the dining car.

This was a Chinese train; at the end of every car was a compartment housing a Chinese guard, responsible for handing out the bed linen and stoking the coal stove that fuelled the samovar from which passengers could take hot water. The guards also used the stove to cook their own food, which they brought with them for the weeks-long journey to Moscow and back, ensuring a supply of stir-fried vegetables and rice even here on the inhospitable steppe.

But the dining car was a little piece of Mongolia. I found it busy, with thick-set staff dispensing meat and potatoes and bottles of vodka to large, appreciative groups.

I could pick out the Mongolians, who were in the majority, instantly. Apart from anything else, they all seemed to be wearing camel-wool sweaters. Most were family groups or bands of young men, whom I guessed were traders travelling to Beijing or to the Chinese border town of Erlian.

A ruddy-faced, camel-hair-clad young man indicated an empty chair at his table, and I sat down. His name was Dorj, and he was a trader, like many others on this train, making one of his regular trips to Erlian, border boomtown, to buy up crates of assorted goods that he'd take back and sell in Ulaanbaatar's markets.

This was the bedrock of the new Mongolian economy. It was not a sophisticated business.

'What do you buy?' I asked.

'All sorts of things,' he said. 'Beer and cigarettes, of course, but also food, shoelaces, toys – in Mongolia we need everything.'

I didn't say it, but I thought he looked too bluff and guileless to be a canny businessman. I had heard that Chinese traders often laughed at their Mongolian counterparts, who would buy anything and hadn't a clue how to drive a hard bargain.

'Can you speak Chinese?'

He laughed shyly. 'I can say "Cheaper, cheaper!"'

'And you bring it all back on the train? Isn't there a limit to how much you can bring in?'

'Oh, no,' he said. 'Whatever we can carry.'

This wasn't entirely true. While Mongolia had abolished import duties on most goods, alcohol and cigarettes were still subject to tariffs, and China imposed export duties. On a previous trip from Beijing to Ulaanbaatar – on a Mongolian train that time – I'd witnessed a fine display of teamwork at the border crossing. As we pulled into the last town on the Chinese side, dozens of Mongolians leapt off the train even before it had stopped. They returned several minutes later lugging crates of beer and cigarettes, which the train guards helped them to conceal under beds and floorboards. When the Chinese customs guards came on, the power failed. Their complaints to the train staff were met with polite, uncomprehending shrugs.

'Is there a lot of money in it?' I enquired.

Dorj shrugged. 'You have to live.'

Our eyes were drawn to the window by a rare glimpse of human activity. A pair of strapping young herders on horseback were racing the train, waving their porkpie hats in the air and laughing. They looked as easy and at home as humans can look, the very essence of Mongolness.

Yet thousands of Mongolians were now in the same business as Dorj, the ubiquitous import-export trade. A few grew rich; most just survived. None of these rough and seemingly unsophisticated people showed the slightest trepidation at wading into the deep and unknown waters of capitalism or at travelling to a foreign land with an unfamiliar language and an endless supply of business savvy.

It always made me wonder. But I recalled a Mongolian proverb that I'd often heard: 'If you're afraid, don't do it. If you do it, don't be afraid.'

Wandering the corridors later, I saw some of the other inhabitants of our little community. There were young Mongolian women – mostly heard as whispers and giggles from behind compartment doors – who'd appear now and then to go to the toilet or to get hot water for their tea. Many were returning to Beijing after visiting their families. There is a large number of Mongolian prostitutes in Beijing; among the sleazier brand of expats, they have a reputation for being – how shall I put this? – good value for the money.

There were a few smart young Mongolian professionals, several of whom I knew, going down to Beijing on shopping holidays or heading off on scholarships abroad. A band of Norwegian travellers whose rolling gait and unruly hair revealed they'd been on the train since Moscow (actually since Oslo – a whole week). Assorted expat residents off to Beijing for R & R, among them several Peace Corps volunteers and a respected conservationist, an expert on the rare snow leopard of the Altai Mountains.

Here we all were, rolling toward China, toward the twenty-first century.

I strolled back to my compartment. It was a four-berth affair – two up, two down – occupied as well by a pair of women in their twenties (sisters, I guessed) and a daughter of about nine. I settled down to read for a while. It was a warm and convivial scene, all laughter and sharing of biscuits. The young girl swung and dangled gymnastically from the bars on the top bunk.

It was still very much a part of Mongolia. Up and down the train, people kept their compartment doors open, strolling to and fro to visit or to make endless cups of tea. It was all so comforting that I fell asleep.

I was jarred awake to bright lights, a great stamping in the corridors and a rapping at the door. The Chinese border guards, swimming in their vast peaked caps and oversized uniforms. They were polite and attentive to me, brusque to my Mongolian travelling companions, who betrayed no hint of annoyance. Then there was an interval, long enough to doze off as the train began to move again – until the lull was shattered by an orgy of creaks and shudders and bangs and a stomach-churning feeling of weightlessness.

I jerked upright and pressed my face against the window. We were in a gigantic shed, rising slowly off the floor. Several other carriages from our train sat alongside; I could see other faces peering from identical windows. Our mighty train was scattered about like a model set, and around it laboured an army of overalled Chinese workers, many of them women. With amazing speed – and a great deal of noise – each carriage was jacked up and its wheels and undercarriage deftly disengaged, rolled away and replaced. Then the cars were shunted, jerked and shuddered back together into a neat line. It took no time at all. It was easily the most efficient thing I'd seen in two years.

The operation, I learned – trainspotters take note – is called changing the bogeys. It had to be done to every train that crossed this border, because ever since the Sino-Soviet rift, China and the Soviet bloc had used different railway gauges. Indeed, there had been no rail service at all between China and Mongolia for several decades.

Soon we were moving again, slowly at first and then faster, away from Mongolia, with that gentle railway roll that always makes me overwhelmingly sleepy.

When I awoke, I looked out the window onto a different planet. There were people everywhere – so that's where they all went! – and, apart from the people, everything was black. The earth. The sky. The smoke from the chimneys and the bricks of the buildings. We were pulling into a station in a world made out of coal. It was piled in heaps by the side of the tracks and spilled over the brims of open-topped railcars. I looked at the station sign. Datong, it said.

I don't want to pass judgement on Datong, a northern Chinese industrial city of several million. It may have its charms – you always see the grubby backside of a city from a train. But it made me heartsick to look at it then.

We pulled out of the city, and things brightened up a bit. Now the world was brown. Brown air. Houses of brown mud. Brown donkeys and olive-clad peasants ploughing brown fields. And still people everywhere: working, walking, cycling.

I couldn't deal with it. I fled to the dining car. But it, too, was a different world. The reassuringly ugly green and orange decor and the smell of grease had gone. In their place were white tablecloths and chopsticks, rice and vegetables, and clear tea. Chinese passengers ate with a deft chorus of clicks. The few Mongolians in the room eyed their plates with suspicion. The dining car had been changed at the border. We were on Chinese territory now.

I walked back to my compartment. The Mongolians who had not disembarked at the border remained behind closed doors. Hitherto unseen Chinese travellers had emerged in their undershirts to take exercise in the corridors. In a few hours, we would be in Beijing.

A slight, middle-aged Chinese man had emerged from the compartment next to mine and stood stretching by the window. I nodded hello.

'Good morning,' he said in English. 'Where do you come from?'

'Canada,' I said.

'Ah! I lived in Canada for many years. Do you know Timmins?'

'By reputation only,' I said.

'Very nice place,' he said with a vigorous nod.

'Are you coming from Ulaanbaatar?' I asked. It was rare enough to meet a Chinese on Mongolian soil.

'Yes. I have been visiting a mine. I am a mining engineer.'

'And how did you find Mongolia?'

A twitch of sadness crossed his face.

'It's like the nineteenth century,' he said with a slow shake of his head. 'It is so very hard to get anything done. It takes so long, so long. Have you been in Mongolia long?'

'Two years.'

He shook his head. 'You should go to Timmins. Much better.'

We rolled on, through decades, it seemed, rather than just miles. From peasants in the fields to smoke-spewing industrial complexes, then a spidery tangle of modern motorways. And billboards, the brightest things on the landscape. The Mongolians were packing up their things. The train turned up a siding, ploughed through a long tunnel, and came to rest at a small station at the foot of the Great Wall.

It was a ten-minute courtesy stop for photo opportunities. People staggered down from the train, stretching their legs and craning their necks. The wall looked remarkably neat and new, as if it had only just been completed. There was no awe-inspiring sense of antiquity. But the size of the project was humbling. It snaked to the horizon in both directions, up and down the peaked backs of the steep hills, studded at every summit by a square guard tower.

An attractive young Mongolian woman in jeans and a camel-hair vest stood beside me and gazed for a moment in silence. 'That was built to keep the Mongols out,' she said. There was quiet pride in her voice.

Mongolians may never feel easy with their southern neighbour. There is too much past there. But they know that a relationship with China is their future; the economic relationship will grow. Although there remains a great deal of respect for Russian culture, Russia is, for now, the past. And the West – it is the future, too, though Mongolians may increasingly wonder what they are getting from the relationship. China will make them richer than the IMF and the World Bank; they will have to deal with this fact. Like most peoples, what they most fear is losing their identity, and in this dizzying time that fear will grow; it may lead to an insularity that, as economics tugs in the other direction, will cause instability. But they are a brave people, with an easy way with strangers and a strong sense of themselves. If they can hang on to these, they may be all right.

We rattled for ages through the suburbs of Beijing: dusty streets and miles of blocks of flats just as drab as the ones in Ulaanbaatar but taller. And painted billboards for a vast array of goods, imported and domestic. And suddenly we were in a real city, passing beside a six-lane expressway and below neon and gleaming skyscrapers.

And then we were in the station. The Mongolians clumped down from the train, heaving baggage, and stood for a moment to get their bearings; then they set off with a resolute gait. At first I could see a few, big-shouldered among the throng. But soon they were lost in the crowd.

I have often missed Mongolia and hope I always will. I miss things that sound like guidebook clichés: the vast sky and soul-stirring open spaces and easy hospitality. It's harder to miss Ulaanbaatar, a city of elusive charms. But I have discovered that it is possible. I have a sensory memory sometimes, a sort of flashback: warm afternoon light, a crisp dry-leaf smell, a luminous blue sky, and the sun shining on the pink stucco of the Mongol Bank building as I walk up the road to Millie's.

Trans-Siberia
Inside the Grey Area
by Paddy Linehan

£8.00 • Paperback • 1 84024 114 4 • 129 x 198 mm/320 pp

'…Mapmakers in general display a distinct prejudice. Europe is planted on the middle of the pages and coloured vibrantly; pinks, blues and duck-egg greens. But when you venture East, things turn spooky. Colours become muddy, borders doubtful and names rare…'

It all started in the mind of a child with the desire to travel. Siberia was full of darkness, struggle, cold and desperation. Years later, haunted by a shadowy image that he just can't shake off, Paddy Linehan decides to pursue his Siberian dream. He learns to think on his feet and travels 'like a Russian' in a culture struggling with post-Soviet, post-communist flux.

Traditional post-bath beatings, bonding with a love-sick Siberian boy, bizarre occurrences on the 44A Trans-Siberian train: this is an extraordinary and very human journey.

'…very cold and very far…' You almost want to go there yourself. Almost.

Empire of the Soul
by Paul William Roberts

£7.99 • paperback • 1 84024 188 8 • 129 x 198 mm/352 pp

'An outrageously funny, brilliantly penetrating and deeply affectionate portrait of India.'   *Martin Amis*

'India is a harsh mistress: she seems to appreciate individual sacrifice so little. Yet she has never wanted for lovers . . .'

India demands a passionate response. In 1974 Paul William Roberts embarked on the first of many trips that began a lasting affair with the country. Spanning twenty years of travel, Roberts paints a picture of a place of constant change, of polarities and extremes, of holy men and millionaire drug dealers, of desperate poverty and riches beyond compare. With characters as diverse as the founder of India's first pornographic magazine to Mother Teresa, *Empire of the Soul* is a seductive, witty and truly unforgettable book.

The Nomad
The Diaries of Isabelle Eberhardt
Translated by Nina de Voogd
Edited by Elizabeth Kershaw and introduced by Annette Kobak

£6.99 • paperback • 1 84024 140 3 • 129 x 198 mm/208 pp

The fascinating story of a strange, passionate life.

In 1904 and at the age of only 27, Isabelle Eberhardt drowned in the deserts of North Africa. Buried beneath the rubble and mud that crushed her were found battered leather journals containing the extraordinary tale of her life. The illegitimate child of aristocracts, a 20-year-old Isabelle travelled to Algeria with her mother, who died 6 months after their arrival. Reinventing herself as a man, embracing Arab nomad tribes and their lifestyle, she wandered the Sahara on horseback.

A controversial figure and equally loved and hated, Isabelle's diaries recount her sexual adventures and drug-taking, her conversion to Islam and the mysterious attempt on her life. Experiencing moments of both desperate loneliness and euphoric joy, Isabelle struggles to find her place, her voice as a writer and the true purpose of human existence.

Adrift in China
by Simon Myers

£7.99 • paperback • 1 84024 217 5 • 129 x 198 mm/320 pp

'In such an extraordinary country it is easy to get lost.'

Time is needed to unravel the mysteries of China, a country holding a quarter of the world's population and with a recorded history going back more than 3,000 years. Simon Myers spent over six years in the Middle Kingdom: firstly as a student, then as a businessman selling the ultimate capitalist icon, Coca-Cola, to the Communists, and finally as an independent traveller on the road on a Chinese motorbike and sidecar. *Adrift in China* is an informed, amusing and personal account that sidesteps the clichés and provides a different take on life at the heart of a fascinating and frustrating country.

For a current catalogue and a full listing of Summersdale travel books, visit our website:

www.summersdale.com